HOUSES
CASAS
HÄUSER

HOUSES
CASAS
HÄUSER

KÖNEMANN

Idea and Concept/Idea y concepto/Idee und Konzept: **Paco Asensio, Hugo Kliczkowski**

Editor and Texts/Editor y textos/Verlagskoordination und Text: **Alejandro Bahamón**

Introduction/Introducción/Einleitung: **Hugo Kliczkowski**

Art Direction/Directora de arte/Art Direktor: **Mireia Casanovas Soley**

Layout/Maquetación/Grafik Design: **Ignasi Gracia Blanco, Cris Tarradas**

English translation/Traducción al inglés/Übersetzung ins Englische: **Michael Brunelle, Beatriz Cortabarria**

Spanish translation/Traducción al español/Übersetzung ins Spanische: **Marta Casado**

German translation/Traducción al alemán/Übersetzung ins Deutsche: **Susanne Engler**

Editorial project/Proyecto editorial/Verlagsprojekt:

© **LOFT** Publications
Via Laietana 32, 4° Of. 92
08003 Barcelona. Spain
Tel.: +34 932 688 088
Fax: +34 932 687 073
loft@loftpublications.com
www.loftpublications.com

© 2005 Tandem Verlag GmbH
KÖNEMANN is a trademark and an imprint of Tandem Verlag GmbH.

ISBN: 3-8331-1588-2

Printed in Italy

10 9 8 7 6 5 4 3 2 1
X IX VIII VII VI V IV III II I

Summary

Índice

Inhalt

8 Introduction

14 HOUSES

16 **Gama-Issa House**

28 **City Hill House**

38 **House in Honda**

50 **Beach House**

60 **Casa Larga**

70 **House in Miravalle**

82 **Castor Packard House**

92 **May Residence**

100 **C-House**

110 **Fung + Blatt House**

120 **Du Plessis House**

130 **Las Encinas Residence**

142 **Double-L**

154 ATTICS

156 **Phillipps / Skaife Residence**

168 **Abbot Kinney Lofts**

180 **Brooklyn Loft**

190 **Vertical Loft**

200 **House in Kuessnacht**

210 **Shoreditch Conversion**

220 **Residence in Gracia**

230 **Motoazabu Housing Complex**

240 **Rooftop**

248 **Ray 1**

258 **Bay Cities Lofts: Phase II**

268 APARTMENTS

270 **Olympic Tower Residence**

278 **House T**

288 **London Mews Conversion**

298 **Flatiron District Loft**

308 **Flexible Loft**

318 **Sempacher Apartments**

328 **Loft in Tribeca**

336 **Small Loft in Vienna**

344 **Lords Telephone Exchange**

354 **House in the Coast**

362 LOFTS

364 **Ling Office and Loft**

374 **Light Loft**

384 **DeBenedetto / Jiang Loft**

392 **TB Guest Loft**

402 **Loft in Soho**

412 **Frank and Amy Loft**

422 **Giobbi / Valentino Residence**

430 **Directory**

© Anriet Denis

"I eagerly search for houses that are 'houses for people' and not houses for architects. It is an important quest. One can say that a house for people emanates love. Allow me to explain this from a filmmaker's point of view: imagine being in a restaurant, not one of those fancy restaurants where the arbitrary intervention of the waiters and the sommeliers destroy my poem, but one of those quaint, small cafés where two or three patrons have just finished drinking their coffees and are chatting.

The plates, glasses, bottles, the salt, the pepper, the napkins, napkin holder... are all still on the table. Observe the total disarray in the relationships between these objects; they have served their purpose, they have all been handled by one guest or another. The distances that separate them represent the measure of daily life. It is a mathematically coherent composition; there is no wrong place in the choice of placement, no hiatus, no false intentions. If a film director who was not contaminated by Hollywood were there at that moment, filming a close up of that still life it would be a testament to pure harmony. Could this be possible? Yes, and how unfortunate are those who seek the false, pretentious, commercial, and academic harmony of Vignola circa 1925, or of the latest fad.

Le Corbusier, in his 1929 American prologue for **Precisions**

"Busco con verdadero afán esas casas que son 'casas de hombres' y no casas de arquitectos. El asunto es grave. Puede decirse que una casa de hombres es amor. Dejadme precisar por esto lo que respecta al cine, observad un día, no en uno de esos restaurantes de lujo, en los cuales la intervención arbitraria de los camareros y de los "sommeliers" destruye mi poema, observad en una pequeña taberna popular, dos o tres comensales que han acabado de tomar su café y están charlando.

La mesa todavía esta llena de vasos, botellas, platos, la aceitera, la sal, la pimienta, la servilleta y el servilletero, etc. Ved el orden fatal que pone todos estos objeto en relación los unos con los otros; todos han servido; han sido cogidos con la mano de uno o de otro de los comensales, las distancias que los separan son la medida de la vida. Es una composición matemáticamente arreglada; no hay ningún falso lugar, ni un hiatus, ni un engaño. Si un cineasta no alucinado por Hollywood se encontrase ahí, filmando esta naturaleza muerta en 'primer plano' tendríamos un testimonio de pura armonía ¿Es posible? Sí, y desgraciados aquellos que buscan falsas armonías, trucadas, comerciales, armonías académicas de Vignola, de 1925 o de última moda".

Le Corbusier, en el prólogo americano de la edición de 1929 de **Precisiones**

„Ich suche mit großem Eifer nach den Häusern, die "Häuser von Menschen", und nicht Häuser von Architekten sind. Das ist eine wirklich ernste Angelegenheit. Man kann sagen, dass ein Haus von Menschen Liebe ist. Lasst mich deshalb ein Beispiel aus dem Kino anführen. Beobachten Sie einen Tagen, aber nicht in einem dieser Luxusrestaurants, in denen das eigenmächtige Eingreifen der Kellner und der „Sommeliers" mein Gedicht zerstört, sondern eine kleine, beliebte Kneipe, in der zwei oder drei Tischgäste gerade ihren Kaffee beendet haben und sich noch ein wenig unterhalten.

Der Tisch ist noch voller Gläser, Flaschen, Teller, die Ölflasche, das Salz, der Pfeffer, die Servietten, der Serviettenhalter, usw. Betrachten Sie die unausweichliche Ordnung, die alle diese Objekte untereinander haben; alle haben zu etwas gedient, alle wurden von der Hand des einen oder anderen Tischgastes aufgenommen, die Abstände, die zwischen ihnen existieren, sind aus dem Leben gegriffene Maße. Es handelt sich um eine mathematisch angeordnete Komposition, es gibt keinen falschen Platz, keinen Hiatus, keine Täuschung. Falls sich ein Cineast, der nicht von Hollywood geblendet ist, hier befände und dieses Stillleben „im Vordergrund" filmen würde, hätten wir ein Zeugnis der reinen Harmonie. Ist das möglich? Ja, und unglücklich sind die, die nach den falschen Harmonien suchen, den vorgetäuschten, kommerziellen, akademischen Harmonien von Vignola im Jahr 1925 oder der letzten Mode".

Le Corbusier, im Amerikanischen Prolog 1929, **Precisiones**

Books, Houses, Cities, and Architects

Why this book?

Because we like to look at houses and design plans, and we love to edit them. A desire (not always possible) is to attract the interest of the reader. We must confess that after so many years in the publishing profession, we truly do not know how to achieve that. We have some ideas and some convictions as well, and we rely on them. We do not know and we do not expect to find out when and why a person chooses a book and, by chance, decides to take it home. We could imagine that it is to share some dream. And that dream, in this case, is a house, a plan, a living space.

And we ask ourselves:

Is an empty house inviting enough to justify this? Does a space that is not our own stimulate our desire to learn more about it? Can a house, wherever it may be, serve as an inspiration and as a model for a similar one?

Is its cost, even if it does not fit our budget, an obstacle for desiring it, or do we want it precisely because it is unattainable?

Desires, fantasies, ambitions, status symbol or not, houses are central to our dreams, and fundamentally, a basic necessity.

Libros, casas, ciudades y arquitectos

¿Por qué este libro?

Porque nos gusta ver casas y proyectos y nos apasiona editarlos. Un deseo (no siempre posible) es conseguir atraer el interés de los lectores. Podemos confesar que después de tantos años en el mundo editorial, sinceramente, no sabemos cómo se consigue esto. Tenemos algunas ideas, algunas certezas también y por ellas apostamos. No sabemos ni podemos saber cuándo y por qué un lector escoge un libro y se lo lleva —casualmente— a su casa. Podemos pensar que es para compartir algún sueño. Y ese sueño, en este caso, será una casa, un proyecto, un espacio habitable.

Y nos interrogamos:

Una casa que no habitamos, ¿nos invita a hacerlo? Un entorno que no es el nuestro, ¿nos estimula a conocerlo? Una casa, dondequiera que esté, ¿nos interesa como modelo para otras similares? Si el coste no se ajusta a nuestras posibilidades, ¿es un obstáculo para desearla, o por el contrario, la queremos justamente por ser inalcanzable?

Deseos, fantasías, ambiciones, ilusiones, símbolo de posición social o no, las casas son una parte central de nuestros sueños y, básicamente, una necesidad vital.

Bücher, Häuser, Städte und Architekten

Warum dieses Buch?

Da wir uns gerne Häuser und Pläne anschauen, und sie leidenschaftlich gerne veröffentlichen. Unser Wunsch ist es (was nicht immer möglich ist), auch das Interesse der Leser damit zu wecken. Wir müssen aber zugeben, dass wir nach so vielen Jahren in der Verlagswelt eigentlich immer noch nicht wissen, wie man das macht. Wir haben da ein paar Ideen und auch einige Gewissheiten, und auf diese setzen wir. Wir wissen nicht und können nicht wissen, wann und warum ein Leser ein Buch auswählt und es, ganz zufällig, nach Hause mitnimmt. Wir könnten denken, dass vielleicht Träume darin verwickelt sind. Und diese Träume sind in diesem Fall ein Haus, ein Projekt, ein Raum zum Wohnen.

Und wir stellen uns ein paar Fragen:

Ein Haus, in dem wir nicht wohnen, lädt es uns zum darin Wohnen ein? Eine Umgebung, die nicht unsere ist, würden wir sie gerne kennen lernen?

Ein Haus, egal, wo es sich befindet, ist es für uns ein interessantes Modell für andere, ähnliche Häuser? Wenn die Kosten nicht unseren Möglichkeiten entsprechen, ist es ein Hindernis, um es uns zu wünschen, oder wollen wir es im Gegenteil, weil es unerreichbar ist?

Wünsche, Phantasien, Ambitionen, Illusionen, Symbol für die gesellschaftliche Stellung oder nicht, Häuser bilden einen Teil unserer Träume, und vor allen Dingen sind sie lebensnotwendig.

Villa Rotonda © Pino Guidolotti

Villa Rotonda © Pino Guidolotti

Houses, Cities, and Architects

House, can, casa, maison, logis, home, haus, shack, vohnung, building, apartment, loft, penthouse, duplex, residence, etcetera.

Yet another question: is a house a building to live in? "A house is a home", Le Corbusier used to proclaim. He also proposed the idea that a house can be a machine to live in.

A house can be so many other things as well, since it constitutes the unit that, together with other elements, shapes and gives meaning to the urban environment, to the city.

And it is the latter that shapes the character of a house, therefore we ask, do the two interact?

Andrea Palladio (1508-1580) wrote in chapter twelve of his Book II that "a city is nothing more than a large house, and on the other hand, a house is nothing more than a small city."

We live in and inhabit houses, we dream about them, we imagine them, and we think about them as described by the great master Frank Lloyd Wright (1869-1959).

"Thinking is dealing with simplicity, and that means thinking of the whole as a single vision..." And he added in referring to the project, that drawing "five lines where three are sufficient is simply foolish."

But what do those houses look like? Are they like the others? And which others? Different, personal, we know that often they are more than a reflection of our needs. Luckily.

Casas, ciudades y arquitectos

Casa, can, house, maison, logis, home, haus, choza, wohnung, edificio, piso, loft, penthouse, dúplex, vivienda, etcétera.

Más preguntas: ¿es la casa un edificio para habitar? "Una casa es un hogar", nos hacía pensar Le Corbusier, y planteaba que una casa puede ser también una máquina de habitar.

Es, además, otras cosas, ya que la casa se constituye en la unidad que conforma y da sentido, junto a otros programas, a la urbe, a la ciudad.

Y es esta última la que da carácter a la casa. ¿Interactúan ambas?

Andrea Palladio (1508-1580) escribía en en el capítulo 12 de su Libro II "la ciudad no es otra cosa que una casa grande y, por el contrario, la casa es una ciudad pequeña".

Vivimos y habitamos en casas, soñamos, nos imaginamos y pensamos en ellas en el sentido que le asignaba el maestro Frank Lloyd Wright (1869-1959). "Pensar es pactar con la sencillez, y eso significa pensar con una visión única para el conjunto..." Y agregaba refiriéndose al proyecto que trazar "cinco líneas donde tres son suficientes es simplemente una estupidez".

¿Pero cómo son esas casas? ¿Son como las otras? ¿Y qué otras? Distintas, personales, sabemos que muchas veces son algo más que el reflejo de nuestras necesidades. Por suerte.

Häuser, Städte und Architekten

Casa, can, house, maison, logis, home, Haus, choza, Wohnung, edificio, piso, loft, penthouse, duplex, vivienda, usw...

Noch mehr Fragen: Ist ein Haus ein Gebäude zum Wohnen?

„Ein Haus ist ein Heim", ließ uns Le Corbusier denken, und er warf gleichzeitig das Problem auf, dass ein Haus auch eine Wohnmaschine sein kann.

Es kann auch noch etwas anderes sein, da das Haus in einer Einheit entsteht, die zusammen mit anderen Elementen, die Stadt bildet, und ihr Sinn gibt.

Und es ist die Stadt, die dem Haus seinen Charakter verleiht. Gibt es eine Wechselbeziehung zwischen beiden?

Andrea Palladio (1508-1580) schrieb im 12. Kapitel seines 2. Buches „Die Stadt ist nichts anderes als ein großes Haus und, im Gegensatz dazu, das Haus ist eine kleine Stadt".

Wir leben und wohnen in Häusern, wir träumen, wir stellen sie uns vor und wir denken an sie in dem Sinne, den der Meister Frank Lloyd Wright (1869-1959) aufzeigte.

„Denken bedeutet, einen Pakt mit der Einfachheit abschließen, und das bedeutet mit einer einzigen Vision für das Gesamte zu denken..." Und er fügte hinzu, wobei er sich auf die Planung bezog, dass beim Zeichnen, „fünf Linien dort, wo drei ausreichen würden, dies einfach dumm ist".

There are people who wish to live in cities like Priene, conforming to the concepts of geometric regularity of Hipodamo de Mileto, in the transitional era between Classicism and Hellenism?

Or would they like living in houses like those in the Fachada Delta project (1954) or Barrio de Xul Solar (1953), (Óscar Agustín Alejandro Schulz Solari, 1887-1963).

Or prefer the houses in Paris where Juan Gris (José Victoriano González, 1887-1927) used to teach.

Or in the DOM-INO House (1916) by Le Corbusier (Charles Édouard Jeanneret-Gris, 1887-1965), or in his apartment buildings in Marseilles, Nantes-Rezé; Briey-en-Fôret; Berlin-Charlottenburg and Firminy-Vert, applying the laws of harmony of his modular.

Or living in Villa Mairea (1937) by Finnish architect Alvar Aalto (1898-1976).

A book, this book about houses, our houses, the houses that others live in, bordering what could be considered their own parameters, show examples, and perhaps prototypes.

We say prototypes because when we speak of houses we also refer to behaviors, to styles, and ultimately, to culture.

This is especially true if we look at them as lifestyles and customs, the knowledge of an era, a social group. A reader looks at the book and sees the houses: does he or she look at them and see them with the purpose of choosing one, or to learn, by inference, what other people have desired?

Habrá quien desee vivir en ciudades como Priene, siguiendo los conceptos de regularidad geométrica de Hipodamo de Mileto, en aquellas épocas de transición entre la edad clásica y el helenismo.

O en casas como las del proyecto Fachada Delta (1954) o Barrio (1953) de Xul Solar (Óscar Agustín Alejandro Schulz Solari, 1887-1963).

O en las casas de París que enseñaba Juan Gris (José Victoriano González, 1887-1927).

O en la casa DOM-INO (1916) de Le Corbusier (Charles Édouard Jeanneret-Gris, 1887-1965), o en sus unidades habitacionales de Marsella, Nantes-Rezé; Briey-en-Fôret; Berlin-Charlottenburg y Firminy-Vert, dejándose llevar por las leyes armoniosas del modulor.

O vivir en la Villa Mairea (1937) del arquitecto finlandés Alvar Aalto (1898-1976).

Un libro, este libro sobre casas, nuestras casas, las casas que habitan otros, bordeando lo que pueden ser los propios parámetros, exhibe ejemplos, quizás prototipos.

Prototipos, porque cuando hablamos de casas también hablamos de comportamientos, de estilos, en definitiva, de cultura.

Sobre todo si la entendemos como el conjunto de modos de vida y costumbres, de los conocimientos de una época, de un grupo social.

Un lector mira el libro, ve las casas, ¿las mira y las ve con actitud de escoger?, ¿o para saber, deduciendo, qué han deseado otras personas?

Aber wie sind diese Häuser? Sind sie wie die anderen? Und welche anderen? Anders, persönlich, wir wissen, dass sie oft mehr als die Widerspiegelung unserer Bedürfnisse sind. Zum Glück.

Es gibt Menschen, die in Städten wie Priene leben möchten, und die den Konzepten der geometrischen Regelmäßigkeit von Hippodamos von Milet folgen, in jenen Epochen des Übergangs von der Klassik zum Hellenismus.

Oder in Häusern wie die des Projektes Fachada Delta (1954) oder Barrio (1953) von Xul Solar (Óscar Agustín Alejandro Schulz Solari, 1887-1963).

Oder in den Häusern von Paris, die Juan Gris (José Victoriano González, 1887-1927) zeigte.

Oder in dem Haus DOM-INO (1916) von Le Corbusier (Charles Édouard Jeanneret-Gris, 1887-1965), oder in seinen Wohneinheiten in Marseille, Nantes-Rezé; Briey-en-Fôret; Berlin-Charlottenburg und Firminy-Vert, um sich von den harmonischen Gesetzen des Modularen hinreißen zu lassen.

Oder in der Villa Mairea (1937) des finnischen Architekten Alvar Aalto (1898-1976).

Ein Buch, unser Buch über Häuser, unsere Häuser, die Häuser, in denen andere wohnen, das sich dem annähert, was die Parameter selbst sein könnten, zeigt Beispiele, vielleicht Prototypen.

Prototypen, da wir, wenn wir über Häuser reden, auch über Verhaltensweisen, Stile, und letzten Endes über Kultur reden.

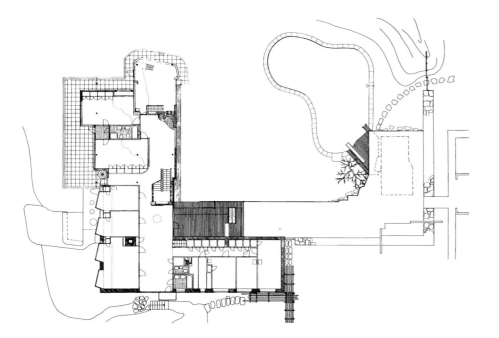

This way, step by step, project by project, house by house, we build a continuum, an understanding of the culture that allows us to learn which house is worth living in and which is not.
And by which architects?

Architects

Oscar Niemeyer (1907) already warned us that he "felt in his heart, that life is more important than architecture. Or that the type of architecture that he preferred was one where courage and freedom of form were essential."
Oscar Niemeyer, by Matthieu Salvaing (HK Publisher). And he had a point when he declared that, "beauty is something that a person is entitled to, because it improves everyone's quality of life."

Alvar Aalto stated at the Architectural Association (AA) conference of 1950 in London that "an architect is someone who manipulates materials and forms; what he says has no value, what he does is what counts."

Hans Hollein (1934) said that for him "architecture is not simply a solution to a given problem, but a kind of opinion."
Houses, we all know, are more than just buildings, they are icons, and as such we display them. Sometimes we show ourselves WITH them, and other times IN them.

Así, paso a paso, proyecto a proyecto, casa a casa, se construye un continuum, un conocimiento de la cultura que nos permite saber qué casa merece ser vivida y cuál no.
¿Y de qué arquitectos?

Arquitectos

Oscar Niemeyer (1907), ya nos advertía de que él "tenía presente en su espíritu, que la vida es más importante que la arquitectura. O que el tipo de arquitectura que prefería era aquel en el que la valentía y la libertad plástica son esenciales".
Oscar Niemeyer, por Matthieu Salvaing (Editorial HK). Y tenía un sentido cuando declaraba que "la belleza es algo a lo que un hombre tiene derecho, ya que mejora la vida de las gentes".

Alvar Aalto afirmaba en 1950 en una conferencia en la Architectural Association (AA) de Londres que "un arquitecto es alguien que maneja los materiales y la forma; lo que diga no vale nada, lo que vale es lo que hace".

Hans Hollein (1934) señala que para él "la arquitectura no es simplemente una solución a un problema dado, sino que es una clase de opinión".
Las casas, ya sabemos, son algo más que construcciones, son iconos, y como tales las mostramos. Muchas veces nos mostramos CON ellas, y otras veces nos mostramos EN ellas.

Vor allem, wenn wir sie als ein Ganzes aus Lebensweisen und Gewohnheiten, den Kenntnissen einer Epoche oder einer sozialen Gruppe verstehen. Ein Leser betrachtet das Buch, er sieht die Häuser. Betrachtet er sie so, als ob er eins aussuchen würde? Oder um zu wissen, um daraus abzuleiten, was andere Menschen sich wünschten?
So wird Schritt für Schritt, Projekt für Projekt, Haus für Haus ein Continuum aufgebaut, ein Wissen um die Kultur, die es uns erlaubt zu wissen, welches Haus es verdient, bewohnt zu werden, und welches nicht.
Und von welchen Architekten?

Architekten

Oscar Niemeyer (1907), sagte uns bereits, dass "es ihm bewusst sei, dass das Leben wichtiger als die Architektur sei. Oder dass die Art von Architektur, die er bevorzugte, die sei, in der der Mut und die gestalterische Freiheit grundlegend sind".
Oscar Niemeyer, von Matthieu Salvaing (Verlag HK). Und es machte auch Sinn, als er erklärte, dass „die Schönheit etwas sei, worauf der Mensch ein Recht hat, da sie das Leben der Menschen verbessert".

Alvar Aalto sagte 1950 auf einer Konferenz der Architectural Association (AA) in London, dass „ein Architekt jemand sei, der mit den Materialien und den Formen umgeht; was er sagt, ist nichts wert, das, was etwas wert ist, ist, was er tut".

Fallingwater House © Paul Rocheleau

As far back as 1919 Walter Gropius (1883-1969) had a vision, to which he assigned a technical name, Bauhaus (house under construction), because he believed that a house was "synonymous with a wealth of ideas, precision in its execution, and capability of adaptation."

A house is an interpretation of life and the surrounding environment, a human and created environment.

Gropius agreed with his peers that a house promotes reflection and the development of future society, when understood in more of an individual context than a social one.

We are what we build, what we live in.

When we look at the projects in this book we smile thinking about classical Greece where artists were famous and well respected, where their personal talents, not their social origins, gave them prestige. Unlike those times, the architects and artists of later Hellenistic periods admitted that their function was more contemplative than practical. The purpose of their art and architecture was to represent reality, not to modify it.

And during the Roman period, the status of artists was even lower, the designer was mistaken for a contractor or an worker, a situation that lasted until the Middle Ages.

Ya en 1919, Walter Gropius (1883-1969) tuvo una visión a la que puso un nombre programático, Bauhaus (casa en construcción), porque pensaba que casa era "sinónimo de riqueza de ideas, exactitud de ejecución y capacidad de adaptación".

La casa como interpretación de la vida y del entorno. Entorno humano y construido.

Gropius acordaba con sus pares que la casa constituía un impulso para la reflexión y el desarrollo futuro de la sociedad, entendida en forma más social que individual.

Somos en tanto que construimos, en tanto que habitamos.

Al ver estos proyectos, nos sonreímos al pensar que en la época clásica, los artistas eran personajes famosos y respetados y que eran sus dotes personales y no su origen social lo que les daba o no prestigio.

A diferencia de los griegos, los arquitectos y artistas del período helenístico reconocen que su función es más contemplativa que práctica, la arquitectura y el arte en el período helenístico sirve para representar la realidad, no para modificarla.

Es en la época romana, donde la consideración social de los artistas es aún más baja, el diseñador se confunde con los constructores o ejecutores y esta situación continúa en la Edad Media.

Hans Hollein (1934) wies darauf hin, dass für ihn „die Architektur nicht nur einfach die Lösung eines gegebenen Problems ist, sondern so eine Art Meinung". Häuser sind, wie wir bereits wissen, etwas mehr als Bauten, sie sind Ikonen, und so zeigen wir sie. Oft zeigen wir uns MIT ihnen, und andere Male zeigen wir uns IN ihnen.

Schon 1919 hatte Walter Gropius (1883-1969) eine Vision, der er einen programmatischen Namen gab, Bauhaus, da er der Ansicht war, dass Haus „gleichbedeutend mit Ideenreichtum, Genauigkeit der Ausführung und Anpassungsfähigkeit" sei.

Das Haus als Interpretation des Lebens und der Umwelt. Menschliche und bebaute Umwelt.

Gropius vereinbarte mit den Seinen, dass ein Haus einen Impuls zum Nachdenken und zur Entwicklung der Zukunft der Gesellschaft sei, das man eher sozial als individuell verstehen sollte.

Wir sind genauso das, was wir bauen, wie das, was wir bewohnen.

Wenn man also die Häuser in diesem Band sieht, lächeln wir bei dem Gedanken, dass im klassischen Griechenland die Künstler berühmte und respektierte Persönlichkeiten waren, und dass es ihr persönliches Talent und nicht ihre gesellschaftliche Herkunft war, das sie berühmt machte.

Im Gegensatz zu jener Zeit erkannten die Architekten und Künstler der späteren, hellenistischen Epoche an, dass ihre Funktion eher kontemplativ als praktisch sei, ihre Architektur und ihre Kunst dienten zur

Fallingwater House © Paul Rochelau

Since this confusion still prevails, the same description would still be valid today.
And thinking about the future, how will it be, what will our books be like, our houses, our cities?

"...nothing that comes from the past can be reborn, but it will never disappear completely either..."

Painters and Masons, Jousimies, 1921

Como esta confusión continúa, uno podría hacer la misma descripción hoy en día.
Y pensar ¿cómo será mañana?, ¿como serán nuestros libros?, ¿nuestras casas?, ¿nuestras ciudades?

"... nada de lo que viene del pasado puede renacer, pero tampoco desaparecerá por completo..."

Painters and Masons, Jousimies, 1921

Darstellung der Wirklichkeit, und nicht dazu, sie zu verändern.
Und in der Zeit der Römer war die gesellschaftliche Anerkennung der Künstler sogar noch geringer. Der Planer wird mit dem Erbauer oder dem Ausführenden verwechselt, diese Situation ändert sich bis zum Mittelalter nicht.

Da diese Verwechslung auch noch weiterhin besteht, könnte man heutzutage die gleiche Beschreibung geben.
Und denken: Wie wird es morgen sein? Wir werden unsere Bücher sein? Unsere Häuser? Unsere Städte?

„...nichts, was aus der Vergangenheit kommt, kann wieder geboren werden, aber es verschwindet auch nicht vollständig..."

Painters and Masons, Jousimies, 1921

Hugo Alberto Kliczkowski Juritz

HOUSES
CASAS / HÄUSER

Gama-Issa House

City Hill House

House in Honda

Beach House

Casa Larga

House in Miravalle

Castor Packard House

May Residence

C-House

Fung + Blatt House

Du Plessis House

Las Encinas Residence

Double-L

This house is located in the Alto de Pinheiros area of the Brazilian city of São Paulo. According to the architect, São Paulo is possibly the least attractive city in the world, a large urban complex where chaos and disorder reign, and where the architecture is almost always unrelated to its setting. This project is no exception; it takes the form of a large white perimeter wall that wraps around the property, isolating it from its context and creating its own views facing the house. The clients are a couple working in the field of advertising, and early in the process they specified the things that should drive the design project. These included a very large shelf that would occupy the double-height living room, large-scale windows that open to the garden, a long swimming pool, a kitchen complete with an orange dining table in the center, two symmetrical marble stairways framed by natural light, a custom-designed studio; and sophisticated spaces with elegant proportions that are permanently linked with the exterior.

Gama-Issa House

Marcio Kogan

São Paulo, Brazil, 2001
Photos © Arnaldo Pappalardo

Esta casa se localiza en la zona de Alto de Pinherios, en la ciudad brasileña de São Paulo que, según el propio arquitecto, es quizás la ciudad menos bella del mundo. Un gran complejo urbano en el que reina el caos y el desorden, por lo que pocas veces un proyecto arquitectónico establece algún diálogo con su entorno. El caso de este proyecto no es una excepción, se trata de un gran envoltorio blanco en forma de muro perimetral que aísla la

Dieses Haus befindet sich im Viertel Alto de Pinheiros in der brasilianischen Stadt São Paulo, die, wie der Architekt sagt, vielleicht die hässlichste Stadt der Welt ist. Eine riesige Stadt, in der Chaos und Unordnung herrschen und in der nur sehr selten die architektonische Planung im Dialog mit der Umgebung steht. Der Fall dieses Gebäudes ist somit keine Ausnahme. Es handelt sich um eine große, weiße Hülle in Form einer Mauer, die das Haus von seiner

propiedad del contexto en el que se ubica para crear un propio paisaje hacia el que se vuelca la casa. Los clientes, una pareja que trabaja en el sector de la publicidad, planteó desde un principio el programa que debía solucionar el proyecto: una estantería de grandes dimensiones que ocupara toda la sala de estar con techos a doble altura, ventanales de gran formato que se abren al jardín, una piscina longitudinal, una cocina que albergara una mesa de comedor naranja en el centro, dos escaleras simétricas de mármol demarcadas por la luz natural, un estudio diseñado a medida y, en general, espacios sofisticados, de proporciones elegantes que se relacionan permanentemente con el exterior.

Umwelt isoliert. Innerhalb dieser Mauern wird eine eigene Landschaft geschaffen, die sich bis zum Haus erstreckt. Die Kunden, ein Paar, das im Werbesektor tätig ist, hatten schon von Anfang an sehr genaue Vorstellungen von dem, was sie sich für ihr Haus wünschten: Ein riesiges Regal, das sich über das gesamte Wohnzimmer mit einer Decke in doppelter Höhe erstreckt, große Fenster, die sich zum Garten hin öffnen, einen längs verlaufenden Swimmingpool, eine Küche, in deren Mitte ein orangener Esstisch stehen sollte, zwei symmetrisch verlaufende Marmortreppen, auf die Tageslicht fällt, ein auf Maß gearbeitetes Atelier und im allgemeinen edle Räume in eleganten Proportionen, die ständig mit außen in Verbindung stehen sollten.

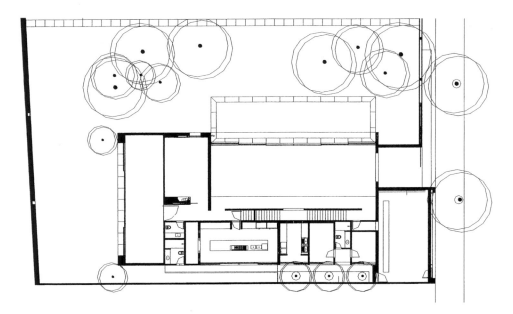

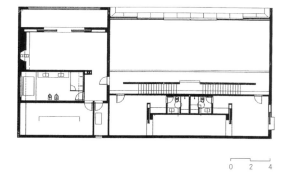

Ground floor

Planta baja

Erdgeschoss

First floor

Planta primera

Erster Stock

Marcio Kogan graduated from the Mackenzie School of Architecture in 1976. Since that time he has received many awards for different architectural assignments. He has designed a variety of small-scale and large-scale projects, mainly in São Paulo, Brazil and the surrounding area. His architectural work is known for its strong, refined lines. Since 1974 he combines architecture projects with his passion for the cinema. He has created a great number of short films, and his first full-length movie was made in 1988.

Marcio Kogan se graduó en la Escuela de Arquitectura Mackenzie en 1976 y desde entonces ha recibido numerosos premios por varias de sus obras arquitectónicas. Ha diseñado una amplia variedad de proyectos de pequeña y gran escala, principalmente en São Paulo, Brasil, y sus alrededores. Su trabajo como arquitecto, en donde destaca una depurada y contundente línea de diseño, lo combina desde 1974 con su pasión por el cine, disciplina en la que ha realizado numerosos cortometrajes y un primer largo en 1988.

Marcio Kogan schloss sein Studium 1976 an der Mackenzie School of Architecture ab und ist seitdem mit zahlreichen Preisen für seine Arbeiten ausgezeichnet worden. Er hat eine ganze Reihe kleiner und großer Gebäude hauptsächlich in São Paulo, Brasilien, und Umgebung entworfen. Seine Arbeit als Architekt ist vor allem von der Klarheit und Überzeugungskraft seiner Entwürfe gekennzeichnet, die er seit 1974 mit seiner Leidenschaft für das Kino kombiniert. Er hat für eine ganze Reihe von Kurzfilmen und auch bereits 1988 für einen Spielfilm Regie geführt.

According to the architects, this house is the result of an in-depth exploration of the different ways of relating to the views — those of the house as well as those that can be seen from it. The project is located on an elevated site with a view of the city of Melbourne on one side and a view of the nearby suburbs on the other. The relevance of these two views is embodied in the house in the form of a break in the large copper façade, which also creates the dramatic feeling of the high interior ceiling. The subtle details of the layout create different kinds of relationships between the various rooms and between the interior and exterior as well. The two-level structure is supported by a large concrete shell, which acts as a base and as a transition to the ground. The pool, the garage, a wine cellar, a storage room, and the access ramp are all located inside this base. The main part of the building, which looks much lighter, is made of a wood and metal frame and very light covering materials that filter the natural light.

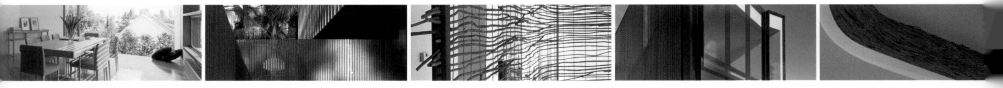

City Hill House

John Wardle Architects

Melbourne, Australia, 2003
Photos © Trevor Mein

Esta casa se convirtió para los arquitectos en toda una exploración sobre las diferentes maneras de relacionar las vistas, tanto de la propia vivienda como las que se extienden fuera de ella. El proyecto se emplaza en un solar elevado que presenta, por un lado, panorámicas de la ciudad de Melbourne y, por el otro, vistas de los suburbios más cercanos. Los ejes de estas dos circunstancias se manifiestan en la volumetría de la construcción en

Mit diesem Gebäude erforschten die Architekten verschiedene Methoden, um den Ausblick zu integrieren, sowohl innerhalb als auch außerhalb des Hauses. Das Gebäude befindet sich auf einem erhöhten Grundstück mit einem ausgezeichneten Blick über die Stadt Melbourne auf der einen Seite und auf die Vororte der Stadt auf der anderen. Die Achsen dieser beiden Faktoren wurden in der Volumetrie des Gebäudes so

forma de una abertura ejecutada en la gran fachada revestida de cobre, que al mismo tiempo determina el carácter dramático de la doble altura interior. Los sutiles giros que presenta la composición general crean diferentes tipos de relaciones entre las diferentes estancias así como entre el interior y el exterior. La estructura de dos plantas está apoyada sobre una vasta envoltura de hormigón que sirve de base y volumen transitorio con el terreno. En esta base se ubican la piscina, el garaje, una bodega, el almacén y la rampa de acceso. El volumen principal, de aspecto mucho más ligero, está formado por una estructura de metal y madera que sirve de marco a revestimientos muy ligeros que filtran la luz natural.

umgesetzt, dass ein Bruch in der großen, mit Kupfer verkleideten Fassade entsteht, die gleichzeitig der doppelten Höhe im Inneren ihren dramatischen Charakter verleiht. Die leichten Drehungen im Gesamtbild schaffen verschiedene Beziehungen zwischen den einzelnen Räumen und zwischen innen und außen. Die zweistöckige Struktur stützt sich auf eine große Betonschale, die gleichzeitig die Basis und der Durchgang auf dem Grundstück ist. Darin befinden sich der Swimmingpool, die Garage, ein Weinkeller, ein Lagerraum und eine Zugangsrampe. Der Hauptteil des Gebäudes wirkt viel leichter und besteht aus einer Holz- und Metallstruktur, die als Rahmen für sehr leichte Verkleidungen dient, durch die sich das Tageslicht filtert.

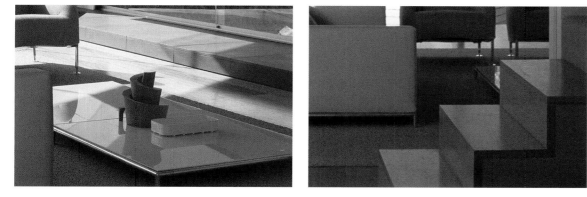

  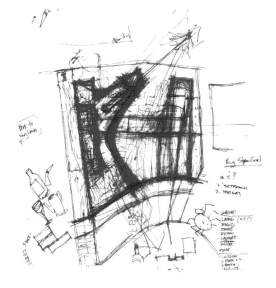

0   10   20

Ground floor

Planta baja

Erdgeschoss

First floor

Planta primera

Erster Stock

Sketch

Croquis

Skizze

1. What historical reference in particular inspires you when designing a residence?
¿Qué referente histórico en particular le sirve de fuente de inspiración a la hora de proyectar una vivienda?
Welche historische Referenz dient Ihnen als Inspiration beim Entwurf eines Hauses?

2. What is the main factor taken into consideration when designing a residence?
¿Cuál es el principal factor determinante a la hora de diseñar una vivienda?
Welche Rahmenbedingungen, bzw. Faktoren sind für Sie ausschlaggebend beim Konzipieren?

3. What room inside the home do you find most interesting to design?
¿Qué estancia de la vivienda encuentra usted más interesante para diseñar?
Welchen Raum des Hauses finden Sie am spannendsten zu entwerfen?

4. What is your criteria for choosing materials and finishings in a particular room?
¿Cuál es su criterio a la hora de seleccionar los materiales y los acabados en esta estancia?
Welche Kriterien wenden Sie bei der Entscheidung über Materialien und Oberflächen in diesem Raum an?

---

1. The personal histories of our clients are intertwined with the history of the site, its physical characteristics, the region and its social history.

2. Each client and each site requires a unique response. The stage-management of views is always an important consideration.

3. Common to many of our projects is a notion of interrupting continuous space with devices and objects rather than compartmentalizing with walls.

4. The sensual aspect of materials and finishes, recognising the sense of touch in the process of design and manufacture. We aspire to create buildings that reflect the perception of our physical world in its vast and diverse phenomena, in the aesthetic experience of surface.

---

1. Las historias personales de nuestros clientes se entrelazan con la historia del lugar, sus características físicas, la región y su historia social.

2. Cada cliente y cada lugar requiere una única respuesta. El manejo de las visuales, por ejemplo, es una consideración importante.

3. Un rasgo común de nuestros proyectos es la noción de un espacio continuo e interrumpido por mecanismos y objetos, más que creando compartimentos con paredes.

4. El aspecto sensual de los materiales y los acabados y reconocer el sentido del tacto en el proceso de diseño y fabricación. Nosotros aspiramos a crear edificios que reflejen la percepción de nuestro mundo físico y su vasta diversidad de superficies.

---

1. Die persönliche Geschichte unserer Kunden verflechtet sich mit der Geschichte des Ortes, seinen physischen Eigenschaften, der Region und ihrer sozialen Geschichte.

2. Jeder Kunde und jeder Ort braucht eine einzige Antwort. Zum Beispiel der Umgang mit der Sicht, sowohl drinnen als auch draußen, ist ein wichtiger Gesichtspunkt.

3. Ein gemeinsamer Zug unserer Projekte ist die Vorstellung eines durchgehenden Raumes, der eher von Mechanismen und Objekten unterbrochen, als dass er durch Wände eingeteilt wird.

4. Das sinnliche Aussehen der Materialien und Oberflächen, wobei der Tastsinn im Gestaltungs- und Herstellungsprozess eine Rolle spielt. Wir versuchen, Gebäude zu schaffen, die unsere Wahrnehmung der physischen Welt und die große Vielfalt an Oberflächen widerspiegeln.

John Wardle Architects was founded in 1986, and at the present time it includes 21 professionals from diverse disciplines who collaborate on developing ideas for each project. The firm's uniqueness stems from the variety of projects that it has undertaken all over Australia. Their design portfolio includes single-family homes, apartment towers, university buildings, offices, and shopping malls. The architects work at incorporating the collective and individual characteristics of their clients to enrich and personalize every project.

La firma John Wardle Architects, fundada en 1986 por el propio Wardle, se compone en la actualidad de 21 profesionales que colaboran en diversas disciplinas para desarrollar las ideas que reciben de cada encargo. La particularidad de la compañía radica en la amplia variedad de escalas de proyectos que llevan a cabo por toda Australia. Su obra abarca casas unifamiliares, torres de apartamentos, edificios para universidades, oficinas y centros comerciales. Las características colectivas y particulares de cada cliente se aprovechan para enriquecer y personalizar cada proyecto.

Das Unternehmen John Wardle Architects wurde 1986 von Wardle selbst gegründet. Heute arbeiten 21 Fachleute verschiedener Disziplinen in diesem Büro, die gemeinsam Projekte entwickeln. Was dieses Unternehmen so besonders macht, ist die Tatsache, dass es in ganz Australien bereits sehr verschiedenartige Planungen durchgeführt hat. Dazu gehören Einfamilienhäuser, Mehrfamilienhäuser, Universitätsgebäude, Bürohäuser und Einkaufszentren. Die kollektiven und individuellen Eigenschaften jedes Kunden werden dazu benutzt, die einzelnen Projekte persönlicher zu gestalten und zu bereichern.

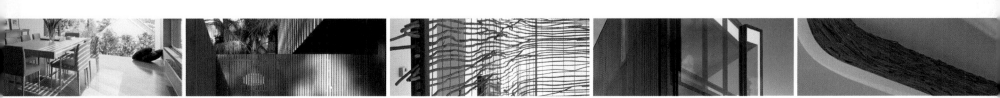

This house is located in Honda, Colombia. This dwelling is a combination of two properties facing the street that used to house residential and storage buildings. Only the façades and a few colonial period stonewalls were preserved and incorporated into the project. The climate is very hot year round because the city is at sea level and in the tropical zone. This second home for three associates was conceived as a sequence of open, covered spaces located inside the existing structure. The floor plan is based on sight lines, which convey a labyrinth-like feeling. Every room faces one of the exterior areas, each representing a particular theme: a patio with aromatic herbs, a garden of citrus trees, a rock garden, and a patio with red peppers. Water acts as a unifying element, in the form of a pool, a fountain, or a pond. The lighting, designed by Guillermo Arias, is a key element of the project, enhancing the character of the original walls, the textures, the vegetation, and the water elements.

House in Honda

Guillermo Arias + Luis Cuartas

Honda, Colombia, 2003
Photos © Eduardo Consuegra

Esta vivienda, situada en Honda, Colombia, está formada por la unión de dos parcelas que contenían antiguamente viviendas y almacenes que daban a la calle. Sólo se conservaban las fachadas y algunos muros coloniales de piedra que se incorporaron en el proyecto. Por estar casi a nivel del mar y en una zona tropical, el clima presenta temperaturas muy elevadas durante todo el año. Esta segunda residencia para tres socios fue concebida como

Dieses Gebäude befindet sich in Honda, Kolumbien. Dieses Haus entstand durch die Vereinigung zweier Parzellen, auf denen sich einst Wohn- und Lagerhäuser zur Straße hin befanden. Nur die koloniale Fassade und die Steinmauern sind erhalten und wurden in die Planung miteinbezogen. Da sich das Gebäude beinahe auf Höhe des Meeresspiegels und in einer Region mit tropischem Klima befindet, ist die Temperatur das ganze Jahr über

una secuencia de espacios abiertos y cubiertos, desarrollados a partir de la estructura encontrada, generando una sensación laberíntica pero ordenada a través de ejes visuales. Los espacios están enfocados siempre hacia algún espacio exterior con un carácter específico: un patio de hierbas aromáticas, un jardín de cítricos y otro de piedras o un patio de ajíes. El agua sirve como elemento unificador, en forma de piscina, fuentes o estanques. La iluminación, a cargo de Guillermo Arias, es un elemento determinante en el proyecto para subrayar el carácter de los muros originales, las texturas, la vegetación o los elementos de agua.

sehr hoch. Dieses Ferienhaus für drei Gesellschafter wurde als eine Sequenz von offenen und geschlossenen Räumen entworfen, die auf der bereits vorhandenen Struktur beruhen. So hat man das Gefühl, sich in einem Labyrinth zu befinden, das über visuelle Achsen geordnet ist. Alle Räume sind auf einen Gartenbereich mit spezifischem Charakter hin ausgerichtet: ein Innenhof mit Duft- und Würzkräutern, ein Garten mit Orangen- und Zitronenbäumen, ein Steingarten und ein Hof voller Pfeffersträucher. Das Wasser dient als vereinigendes Element, in Form eines Swimmingpools, eines Brunnens und eines Teiches. Die Beleuchtung, die von Guillermo Arias entworfen wurde, ist ein entscheidendes Gestaltungselement, das den Charakter der alten Mauern, die Textur, die Vegetation und die Wasser-Elemente unterstreicht.

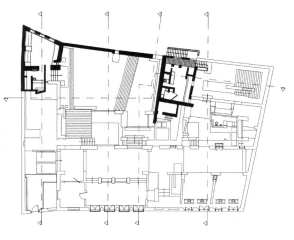

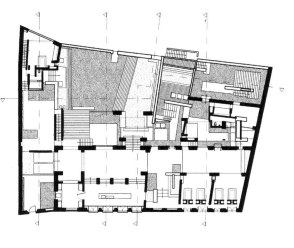

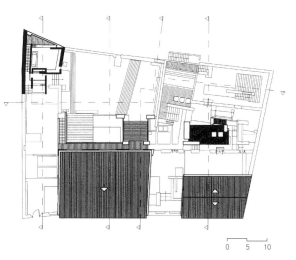

0   5   10

Ground floor

Planta baja

Erdgeschoss

First floor

Planta primera

Erster Stock

Roof plan

Planta de cubiertas

Dachgrundriss

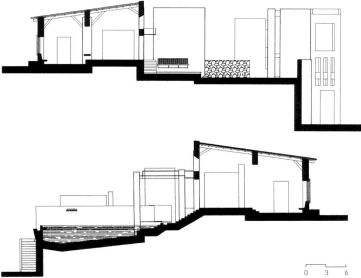

Sections

Secciones

Schnitte

0   3   6

Axonometry

Axonometría

Axonometrie

1. What historical reference in particular inspires you when designing a residence?
¿Qué referente histórico en particular le sirve de fuente de inspiración a la hora de proyectar una vivienda?
Welche historische Referenz dient Ihnen als Inspiration beim Entwurf eines Hauses?

2. What is the main factor taken into consideration when designing a residence?
¿Cuál es el principal factor determinante a la hora de diseñar una vivienda?
Welche Rahmenbedingungen, bzw. Faktoren sind für Sie ausschlaggebend beim Konzipieren?

3. What room inside the home do you find most interesting to design?
¿Qué estancia de la vivienda encuentra usted más interesante para diseñar?
Welchen Raum des Hauses finden Sie am spannendsten zu entwerfen?

4. What is your criteria for choosing materials and finishings in a particular room?
¿Cuál es su criterio a la hora de seleccionar los materiales y los acabados en esta estancia?
Welche Kriterien wenden Sie bei der Entscheidung über Materialen und Oberflächen in diesem Raum an?

1. We do not use specific historic references when designing a residence. We are inspired as much by a Pompeian villa as by a modern house by Neutra or Mies van der Rohe.

2. The location and the requirements are the rational determining factors, while the pursuit of sensibility in the space is our personal approach.

3. The spaces that we consider most interesting are opposites, the most private ones and the ones that are most exposed and public. The former encourage intimacy and contemplation, while the more open living areas are the spatial culmination of the design process.

4. There are several aspects that influence the selection of materials: rational ones like the climate and the availability, and sensory ones like the feeling conveyed by the space.

1. No tenemos referente histórico concreto a la hora de proyectar una vivienda. Para nosotros es igual de inspirador una villa pompeyana que una casa moderna de Neutra o Mies van der Rohe.

2. El lugar y el programa son los factores determinantes racionales, mientras que la búsqueda de la sensibilidad en el espacio se convierte en nuestro objetivo personal.

3. Las estancias que consideramos más interesantes son opuestas: las más íntimas y las más públicas. Las primeras permiten el recogimiento y la contemplación, mientras que las segundas, por ejemplo, las áreas de estar, más abiertas, las entendemos como la conclusión espacial del ejercicio de diseño.

4. Para la selección de un material influyen varios aspectos: los racionales, como el clima y la disponibilidad, y lo sensorial, es decir, lo que el espacio transmite.

1. Wir haben keine konkrete historische Referenz bei der Planung eines Wohnhauses. Uns inspiriert eine pompejische Stadt genauso wie ein modernes Haus von Neutra oder Mies van der Rohe.

2. Der Ort und das Wohnprogramm sind die rationalen Gründe für die Entscheidung, während die Suche nach Sensibilität des Raumes unsere persönliche Suche ist.

3. Die Räume, die wir am interessantesten finden, sind in einer Art Gegenüberstellung die Räume, die am privatesten sind und die, die geteilt und gezeigt werden. In den ersten sucht man die Zurückgezogenheit und die Betrachtung, während in den anderen die Wohnbereiche offener sind. Diese verstehen wie als die räumliche Schlussfolgerung des gestalterischen Eingriffs.

4. Die Materialauswahl wird von verschiedenen Aspekten beeinflusst, rationale Aspekte wie das Klima und die Verfügbarkeit und emotionale Aspekte, die der Raum vermittelt.

Guillermo Arias was born in Bogota, Colombia, and has been an architect at the Universidad de los Andes since 1986. That same year he founded the firm Octubre, where he designs various lighting projects and does architectural work. Since 2002 he has designed lamp collections for Goldsmith in New York.
Luis Cuartas was born in Medellin, Colombia, and has been an architect at the Universidad Javierana since 1990. Since then the two have collaborated on a wide variety of residential and commercial projects.

Guillermo Arias nació en Bogotá, Colombia, y es arquitecto de la Universidad de los Andes desde 1986. En este mismo año fundó la firma Octubre, en donde desarrolla varios proyectos de iluminación paralelamente a su trabajo como arquitecto. Desde 2002 es diseñador de la colección de lámparas para Goldsmith en Nueva York.
Luis Cuartas nació en Medellín, Colombia, y es arquitecto de la Universidad Javeriana desde 1990. Desde entonces, ambos trabajan como arquitectos asociados en una amplia variedad de proyectos residenciales y comerciales.

Guillermo Arias kam in Bogotá in Kolumbien auf die Welt und machte 1986 sein Architekturdiplom an der Universität der Anden. Im gleichen Jahr gründete er das Unternehmen Octubre, in dem er verschiedene Beleuchtungsprojekte parallel zu seiner Arbeit als Architekt verwirklichte. Seit 2002 entwirft er die Lampenkollektion für Goldsmith in New York.
Luis Cuartas wurde in Medellín in Kolumbien geboren und schloss 1990 sein Architekturstudium an der Universität Javeriana ab. Seit diesem Jahr arbeiten die beiden Architekten an zahlreichen Bauprojekten für Wohn- und Geschäftshäuser zusammen.

The clients for this project, a couple with two children, were originally from the Philadelphia area. For the past ten years they have spent their summers on Long Beach Island, an island on the south coast of New Jersey. They were attracted to this property because of its solitary and comfortable character, lent by the area's dense woods. The clients not only wanted to maintain and protect this vegetation, but to make it an integral part of the project so they could enjoy it from within the living areas of the home. These concepts lead to the idea of placing the living quarters of the house on a higher level to create a more direct relationship with the vegetation. The more private areas, like the bedrooms, were placed on an even higher floor, above the trees and with a view of the ocean. The guest room, an office/gym, a storage room, and the building's entrance that faces the woods, are all on the ground floor. A metal framework reinforces the wooden structure and supports the large projections that emphasize the relationship with the surroundings.

Beach House

Christoff:Finio architecture

Long Beach Island, NY, USA, 2003
Photos © Elizabeth Felicella

Los clientes de este proyecto, originarios de la zona de Filadelfia, son una pareja con dos hijos. Esta familia ha pasado los veranos de los últimos diez años en Long Beach Island, una isla situada en la costa sur de Nueva Jersey. Adquirieron esta propiedad atraídos por su carácter solitario y acogedor que les confería el denso bosque que existe en el paraje. Los propietarios no sólo querían respetar y proteger esta vegetación, sino integrarla en el

Die Auftraggeber für dieses Haus stammen aus der Gegend von Philadelphia. Es handelt sich um ein Paar mit zwei Kindern, die während der letzten 10 Jahre den Sommer auf Long Beach Island, einer Insel an der Südküste von New Jersey, verbracht haben. Dieses Haus inmitten eines dichten Waldes sagte ihnen aufgrund der zurückgezogenen und gleichzeitig einladenden Lage zu. Die Kunden wollten diesen Wald nicht nur erhalten und

proyecto y poder disfrutarla desde las áreas de estar de la casa. Esta premisa llevó a la idea de plantear las zonas de estar de la vivienda en un nivel más elevado y así tener una relación más directa con la vegetación. La esfera más privada, como las habitaciones, se sitúa en la segunda planta, por encima de la copa de los árboles y con vistas al mar. En la planta baja se ubica la habitación de huéspedes, una oficina-gimnasio, un almacén y el acceso a la vivienda que se abre al bosque. Una estructura metálica tiene como función reforzar la estructura de madera y sustenta los voladizos que ensalzan la relación con el entorno.

beschützen, sondern ihn auch zu einem integralen Bestandteil der Planung machen, und ihn vom Wohnzimmer des Hauses aus genießen. Dadurch kam den Planern die Idee, die Wohnbereiche des Hauses auf einer etwas höheren Ebene anzulegen, um so eine direkte Beziehung zur Vegetation zu haben. Die privateren Räume wie die Schlafzimmer liegen auf einer noch höheren Ebene, über den Bäumen und mit Blick aufs Meer. Im Erdgeschoss befinden sich das Gästezimmer, ein Büro-Fitnessraum, ein Lager und der Zugang zum Haus, der sich zum Wald hin öffnet. Eine Metallstruktur verstärkt die Holzstruktur und stützt die großen Vorsprünge, die Beziehung zur Umgebung unterstreichen.

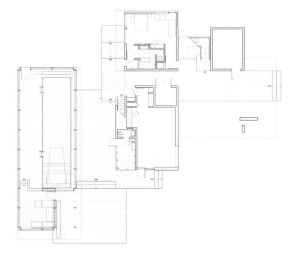

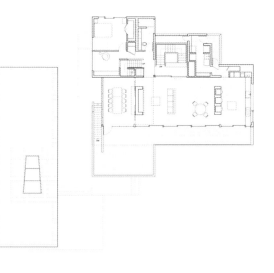

Ground floor

Planta baja

Erdgeschoss

First floor

Planta primera

Erster Stock

Second floor

Planta segunda

Zweiter Stock

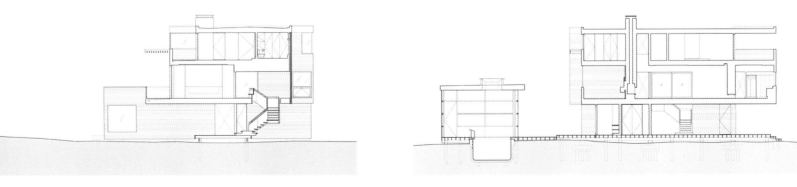

0   2   4

Sections

Secciones

Schnitte

1. What historical reference in particular inspires you when designing a residence?
¿Qué referente histórico en particular le sirve de fuente de inspiración a la hora de proyectar una vivienda?
Welche historische Referenz dient Ihnen als Inspiration beim Entwurf eines Hauses?

2. What is the main factor taken into consideration when designing a residence?
¿Cuál es el principal factor determinante a la hora de diseñar una vivienda?
Welche Rahmenbedingungen, bzw. Faktoren sind für Sie ausschlaggebend beim Konzipieren?

3. What room inside the home do you find most interesting to design?
¿Qué estancia de la vivienca encuentra usted más interesante para diseñar?
Welchen Raum des Hauses finden Sie am spannendsten zu entwerfen?

4. What is your criteria for choosing materials and finishings in a particular room?
¿Cuál es su criterio a la hora de seleccionar los materiales y los acabados en esta estancia?
Welche Kriterien wenden Sie bei der Entscheidung über Materialien und Oberflächen in diesem Raum an?

---

1. The history of domesticity.

2. How to dignify living.

3. Any room that can extend outdoors.

4. Quiet innovation.

---

1. La historia de lo doméstico.

2. Cómo ampliar una vivienda.

3. Cualquier habitación que se abra al exterior.

4. La innovación moderada.

---

1. Die Geschichte der Häuslichkeit.

2. Wie kann man eine Wohnung vergrößern.

3. Alle Räume, die sich nach außen öffnen.

4. Die maßvolle Innovation.

Martin Finio graduated from Cooper Union in New York. For ten years he was an associate architect in the office of Tod Williams and Billie Tsien, where he lead and participated in a wide variety of projects. He was the editor of the monograph "William Tsien: Works", and was a professor at Columbia and Yale Universities.
Taryn Christoff graduated from IIT and worked for several years in New York on large and small-scale projects, gaining experience in both corporate and residential projects. She founded the firm which Martin Finio would later join to create Christoff:Finio architecture.

Martin Finio se graduó en la Cooper Union de Nueva York y fue arquitecto asociado durante diez años en la oficina de Tod Williams y Billie Tsien, en donde lideró y participó en una amplia variedad de proyectos. Ha trabajado como editor en la monografía "William Tsien: Works" así como de profesor en las universidades de Columbia y Yale.
Taryn Christoff se graduó en IIT y trabajó durante varios años en Nueva York en proyectos de gran y pequeña escala ganando experiencia tanto en proyectos corporativos como residenciales. Fundó la firma a la que más tarde se incorporó Martin Finio para crear Christoff:Finio architecture.

Martin Finio studierte an der Cooper Union in New York und war 10 Jahre lang als assoziierter Architekt bei Tod Williams und Billie Tsien tätig, wo er an einer großen Reihe an Projekten teilnahm oder sie leitete. Er arbeitete als Herausgeber der Monographie „William Tsien: Works" und als Professor an den Universitäten von Columbia und Yale. Taryn Christoff schloss seine Studien an der IIT ab und arbeitete mehrere Jahre in New York, wo er Erfahrungen sowohl bei der Planung von Geschäfts- als auch Wohnhäusern sammelte. Er gründete die Firma, der später auch Martin Finio beitrat, und aus der dann Christoff:Finio architecture entstand.

This wood house, located in a rural area where stone is the principal construction material, was inspired by the agricultural buildings of the region. The architect defines the project as a granary for an artist, because the house incorporates a working studio. The goal was to capture the best views of Lake Maggiore, so the building was designed in the form of a tower that was predominately vertical. The structural walls are made of concrete, while the interior walls are fabricated from insulated panels that are lighter and more flexible. The covering on the exterior, composed of narrow wood boards, emphasizes the verticality of the building even more, while a balcony that faces the west acts as a horizontal counterpoint. The location on the highest part of a hill represented a construction challenge, because there was no existing entrance from the highway. As a result of this the architects chose a prefabricated wood structure that was assembled in three days with the help of a helicopter.

Casa Larga

Daniele Claudio Taddei

Kloten, Switzerland, 2001
Photos © Bruno Helbling / zapaimages

Ubicada en una zona rural, en donde se emplea principalmente la piedra como material de construcción, esta
casa de madera se inspira en las construcciones agríco-
las de la región. El arquitecto define el proyecto como un
granero para un artista, ya que se trata de una vivienda
que incorpora un estudio de trabajo. La premisa del proyecto era la de alcanzar las mejores panorámicas del
lago Maggiore, por lo que el volumen se plantea como un

Dieses Holzhaus, das in einem ländlichen Gebiet liegt, in
dem hauptsächlich Steine als Baumaterial verwendet werden, ist von den Bauernhäusern der Region inspiriert. Der
Architekt definiert das Gebäude als eine Scheune für
einen Künstler, da es sich um ein Wohnhaus mit einem
Atelier handelt. Von dem Gebäude aus sollte man einen
der besten Panoramablicke auf den Lago Maggiore genießen, deshalb ist es vertikal wie ein Turm aufgebaut. Die

elemento vertical, en forma de torre. Los muros estructurales están construidos de hormigón, mientras que los
tabiques que dividen el interior están fabricados con
paneles aislantes y permiten una mayor flexibilidad y ligereza. El revestimiento exterior de la fachada, a partir de
listones de madera, ensalzan aún más la verticalidad del
edificio, mientras que un balcón mirador orientado hacia
el oeste, sirve de contrapunto horizontal. El emplazamiento, en la cima de una colina, representó un desafío cons-
tructivo, ya que no existía acceso desde la carretera. En
consecuencia, recurrieron a un sistema prefabricado de
madera que se montó en tres días con la ayuda de un
helicóptero.

tragenden Wände sind aus Beton, während die
Zwischenwände im Inneren aus Isolierpaneelen sind, was
die Gestaltung flexibler macht und dem Haus mehr
Leichtigkeit verleiht. Die Fassade ist von außen mit
Holzlatten verkleidet, was die vertikale Form noch unterstreicht. Ein Aussichtsbalkon mit Blick nach Westen dient
als horizontaler Kontrapunkt. Der Standort oben auf
einem Hügel war eine Herausforderung für die Planer, da
es keine Zufahrt von der Landstraße aus gibt. Deshalb
wurde das Gebäude mit einem Fertighaussystem aus Holz
errichtet, das mit einem Hubschrauber transportiert und
in drei Tagen montiert wurde.

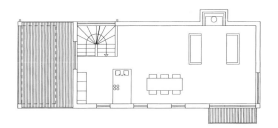

Ground floor

Planta baja

Erdgeschoss

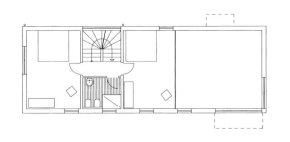

First floor

Planta primera

Erster Stock

Second floor

Planta segunda

Zweiter Stock

 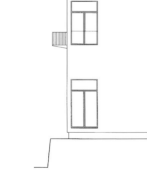 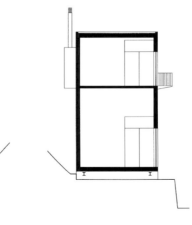 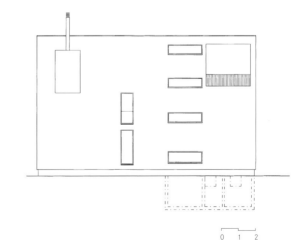

0 1 2

Sections

Secciones

Schnitt

Elevation

Alzado

Aufriss

Daniele Claudio Taddei was born in Lugano, Switzerland, in 1960. He pursued his early studies in Lugano and Tarasp, Switzerland, and continued with advanced studies in Stuttgart, Germany, graduating in 1986. He worked as an architect in several offices in Germany, Italy, the United States, and Switzerland. Since 2001 he has his own firm in Zurich, where he designs a variety of architecture and interior projects.

Daniele Claudio Taddei nació en Lugano, Suiza, en 1960. Después de cursar sus primeros estudios en Lugano y Tarasp, Suiza, continuó sus estudios superiores en Stuttgart, Alemania, en donde se graduó en 1986. Ha trabajado como arquitecto colaborador en varias oficinas de Alemania, Italia, Estados Unidos y Suiza. A partir de 2001 funda su propia firma en Zurich, en donde desarrolla una gran variedad de proyectos de arquitectura y diseño interior.

Daniele Claudio Taddei kam 1960 in Lugan in der Schweiz auf die Welt. Nachdem er sein Studium in Lugan und Tarasp in der Schweiz begonnen hatte, setzte er es in Stuttgart in Deutschland fort, wo er 1986 sein Diplom erwarb. Er arbeitete als Architekt mit verschiedenen Architekturbüros in Deutschland, Italien, in den Vereinigten Staaten und in der Schweiz zusammen. Im Jahre 2001 gründete er seine eigene Firma in Zürich, mit der er eine Vielzahl von Projekten in den Bereichen Architektur und Innenarchitektur durchführt.

The main challenge of this project was designing a house that would take full advantage of the many views, while maintaining the privacy of its occupants and blending in with the surrounding environment. One part of the property faces the Andes mountain range including Cotopaxi, the highest snow-covered active volcano in Ecuador. The architects Wood + Zapata designed a house that was adapted to the site's mountainous terrain. The two main wings of the building form a large angle, allowing them to take in most of the views and create a feeling of proximity. A projecting terrace on the main wing of the house extends from the dining room towards Cotopaxi. The other wing ends at a road that borders the mountain and the swimming pool, which also extends outwards from inside the building. The façade that faces the mountain is almost entirely covered with green-colored glass, so one can always enjoy the view from the inside. From the outside the house blends into the landscape when viewed from across the valley.

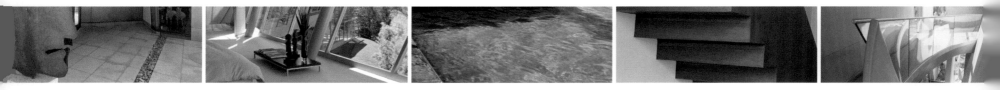

House in Miravalle

Wood + Zapata

Miravalle, Ecuador, 2002
Photos © Undine Pröhl

El mayor reto de este proyecto consistía en diseñar una casa que aprovechara las múltiples ventajas visuales del entorno, pero al mismo tiempo mantuviera la intimidad de sus habitantes y se adaptara al paisaje circundante. Una parte del solar se orienta hacia la cordillera de los Andes con Cotopaxi, el volcán activo nevado de más altitud en Ecuador. Los arquitectos Wood + Zapata diseña-ron la vivienda para que se adaptara a la naturaleza

Die große Herausforderung bei dieser Planung war es, ein Haus zu entwerfen, das die interessante Aussicht inte-griert, aber gleichzeitig die Privatsphäre der Bewohner schützt und sich der Umgebung anpasst. Von einer Seite des Grundstückes sieht man auf die Andenkette und den Cotopaxi, den höchsten aktiven Vulkan in Ecuador. Die Architekten Wood + Zapata haben das Haus an die bergi-ge Landschaft angepasst. Die beiden Hauptflügel des

montañosa del lugar. Las dos alas principales del pro-yecto plantean un amplio ángulo entre ellas y de este modo abarcan la mayor parte de las vistas y se acercan más a ellas. El ala principal de la casa alberga una terra-za en voladizo que se extiende a partir del comedor en eje hacia el Cotopaxi. La otra ala finaliza en un camino que bordea la montaña y en la piscina que se prolonga también desde el interior de la vivienda. La fachada que mira hacia la montaña está casi totalmente revestida de un cristal coloreado de verde, que permite disfrutar per-manentemente de las vistas panorámicas; desde el otro lado del valle, el exterior de la casa es visto como parte integrante del paisaje.

Gebäudes bilden einen weiten Winkel, um die wundervol-le Aussicht näher zu bringen und so weit wie möglich zu umfassen. Der Hauptflügel des Hauses läuft in eine Terrasse auf einem Vorsprung aus, der sich vom Esszimmer in der Achse bis zum Cotopaxi erstreckt. Der andere Flügel endet an einem Weg, der an dem Berg ent-lang führt und am Swimmingpool, der ebenfalls bis in das Innere des Hauses reicht. Die Fassade zum Berg hin besteht fast vollständig aus grünem Glas, so dass man vom Inneren aus ständig diesen überwältigenden Blick hat und von außen, von der anderen Seite des Tales aus betrachtet, verschwindet das Haus fast in der Landschaft.

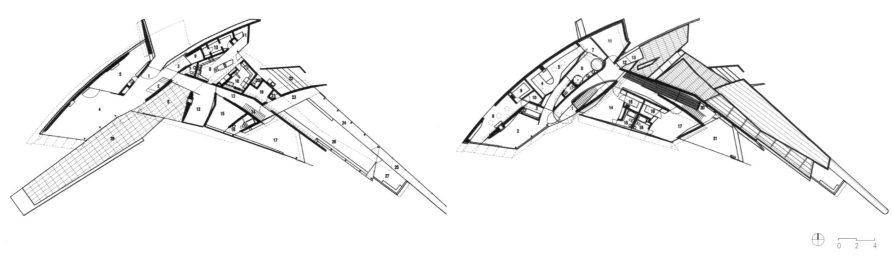

Ground floor

Planta baja

Erdgeschoss

First floor

Planta primera

Erster Stock

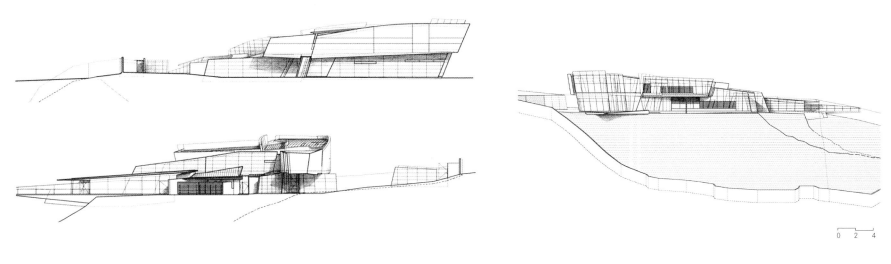

Elevations

Alzados

Aufriss

Section

Sección

Schnitt

1. What historical reference in particular inspires you when designing a residence?

   ¿Qué referente histórico en particular le sirve de fuente de inspiración a la hora de proyectar una vivienda?

   Welche historische Referenz dient Ihnen als Inspiration beim Entwurf eines Hauses?

2. What is the main factor taken into consideration when designing a residence?

   ¿Cuál es el principal factor determinante a la hora de diseñar una vivienda?

   Welche Rahmenbedingungen, bzw. Faktoren sind für Sie ausschlaggebend beim Konzipieren?

3. What room inside the home do you find most interesting to design?

   ¿Qué estancia de la vivienda encuentra usted más interesante para diseñar?

   Welchen Raum des Hauses finden Sie am spannendsten zu entwerfen?

4. What is your criteria for choosing materials and finishings in a particular room?

   ¿Cuál es su criterio a la hora de seleccionar los materiales y los acabados en esta estancia?

   Welche Kriterien wenden Sie bei der Entscheidung über Materialien und Oberflächen in diesem Raum an?

1. There is no particular reference that applies to all residence projects. Obviously, there are masterfully executed houses that are part of the knowledge of every architect, such as the Schindler House, Falling Water, and works by Lautner, however, it is important to reconize the importance that the site has on the particular work.

2. Obviously the client. A custom designed residence should reflect the lifestyle of the person or family who commissions it. Equally important is the site and the climate in which it's built.

3. Each room is an element that completes the composition of the house. It's hard for me to pick one.

4. I use materials as providing color and texture as well as defining relationships between planes, however, in a house or room it is most important to create a warm balance between all the materials.

1. No hay una referencia concreta aplicable a todos los proyectos residenciales. Obviamente, hay casas magistralmente diseñadas que están en la mente de todo arquitecto, como la casa Schindler, la casa de la Cascada y los trabajos de Lautner; sin embargo, es importante reconocer la relevancia que tiene el emplazamiento dentro de un trabajo concreto.

2. El cliente, obviamente. Una casa debe reflejar el estilo de vida de la persona o la familia que encarga el proyecto; es igual de importante el lugar y el clima donde se emplaza.

3. Cada habitación es un elemento que complementa la composición de la casa. Es difícil escoger una.

4. Utilizo materiales que proporcionen color y textura y que definan las relaciones entre los planos; sin embargo, en una casa o una estancia lo más importante es crear un cálido equilibrio entre todos los materiales.

1. Es gibt keine konkrete Referenz, die man auf alle Wohnprojekte anwenden kann. Offensichtlich gibt es perfekt geplante Häuser, an die jeder Architekt denkt, wie das Haus Schindler, und das Haus Wasserfall die Arbeiten von Lautner, dennoch ist es wichtig, an die Bedeutung des Standortes für eine konkrete Planung zu denken.

2. Natürlich der Kunde. Ein Haus sollte den Lebensstil einer Person oder einer Familie, die es sich bauen lässt, widerspiegeln. Das ist ebenso wichtig wie der Standort und das Klima der Umgebung.

3. Jeder Raum ist ein Element, das die Gestaltung des Hauses beeinflusst. Es ist schwierig, einen auszuwählen.

4. Ich benutze Materialien, die Farbe und Textur besitzen und die die Beziehungen zwischen den Ebenen definieren. Dennoch ist es in einem Haus oder einer Wohnung wichtig, ein warmes Gleichgewicht zwischen allen Materialien zu schaffen.

Since its inception in 1996, Wood + Zapata has made an effort to imprint its personal design perspective on each of the many different projects it has completed. These include the Chicago Bears Stadium, several private homes, spaces for commercial use, large-scale residential complexes, the new international terminal at the Miami airport, and the new construction and total rehabilitation of two blocks of the French historic center in Shanghai. From their offices in New York and Shanghai, they work on projects that range from master plans to furniture design.

Desde sus inicios en 1996, la firma Wood + Zapata se ha esforzado por impregnar su personal perspectiva del diseño en cada uno de los variados proyectos que han ejecutado. Entre sus obras se encuentran el estadio Chicago Bears, numerosas casas privadas, proyectos de uso comercial, complejos residenciales de gran escala, la nueva terminal internacional del aeropuerto de Miami y la completa rehabilitación y nueva construcción de dos bloques del centro histórico francés de Shangai. En sus dos oficinas, en Nueva York y Shangai, desarrollan proyectos que comprenden desde planes maestros hasta el diseño de mobiliario.

Seit der Gründung 1996 hat die Firma Wood + Zapata sich stets darum bemüht, ihre persönliche, architektonische Perspektive in jede ihrer Planungen einzubringen. Zu ihren Arbeiten gehören das Chicago Bears Stadium, viele Privat- und Geschäftshäuser, große Wohnkomplexe, das neue, internationale Terminal am Flughafen von Miami und der völlige Um- und Neubau von zwei Häuserblöcken im historischen, französischen Viertel von Shanghai. In ihren Büros in New York und Shanghai entwickeln sie Projekte, die von Masterplänen bis hin zum Möbeldesign reichen.

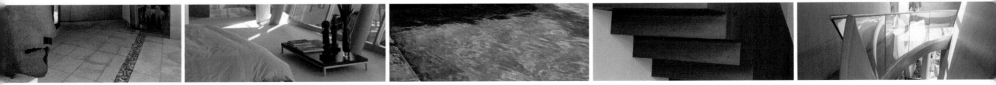

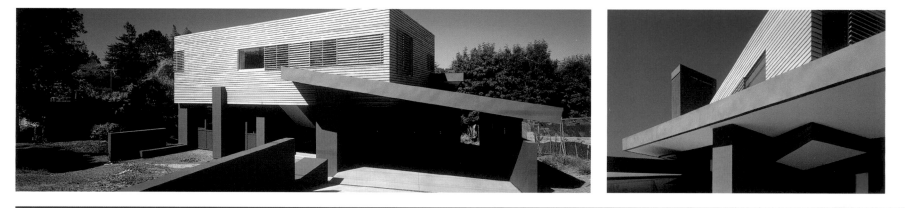

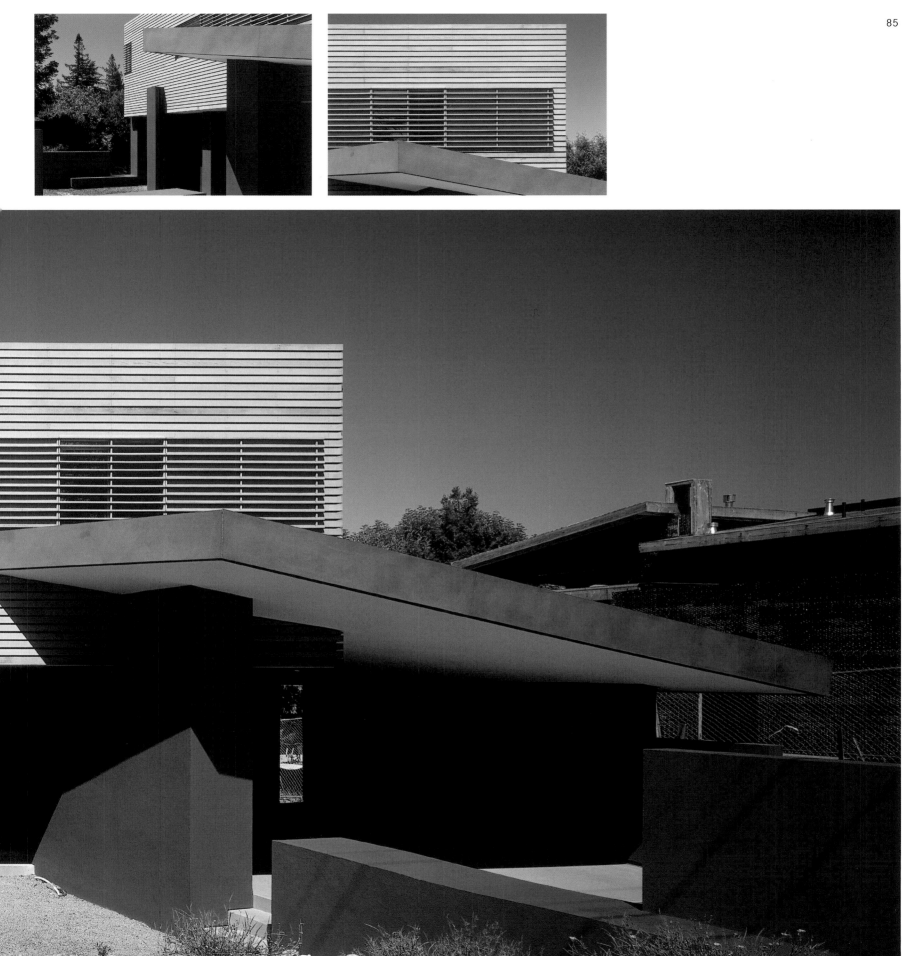

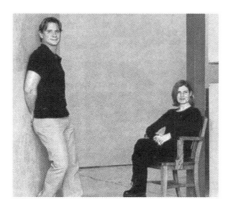

The architectural firm of Callas Shortridge Architects has been in existence since 1996. Their founders, Steven Shortridge and Barbara Callas were architects at Israel Design Associates of Beverly Hills. Before starting their own office, the two worked together as project architects on a wide range of assignments of different scales. Barbara heads the development of projects that require detailed technical knowledge. Steven leads and manages the design and construction process for the firm's different projects. Both have received many prestigious awards for their design work.

La firma Callas Shortridge Architects existe desde 1996. Sus fundadores, Steven Shortridge y Barbara Callas formaron parte como arquitectos asociados de la firma Israel Design Associates, en Beverly Hills. Antes de crear su propia oficina, ambos colaboraron como arquitectos proyectistas desarrollando una amplia variedad de trabajos de diferentes escalas. Barbara lidera el desarrollo de proyectos, lo cuales requieren profundos conocimientos técnicos. Steven dirige y maneja el proceso de diseño y construcción para los diferentes proyectos de la firma. Ambos han recibido numeros premios prestigiosos de diseño por su trabajo.

Callas Shortridge Architects existiert seit dem Jahr 1996. Die Gründer Steven Shortridge und Barbara Callas waren vorher als assoziierte Architekten bei Israel Design Associates in Beverly Hills tätig. Bevor sie ihr eigenes Architekturbüro ins Leben riefen, arbeiteten sie als Projektarchitekten an Planungen verschiedener Größenordnung mit. Barbara überwacht die Projektabwicklung bei Planungen, für die ausgezeichnete technische Kenntnisse notwendig sind. Steven leitet den Gestaltungs- und Bauprozess für die veschiedenen Projekte des Unternehmens. Beide erhielten für ihr Werk bereits wichtige Designpreise.

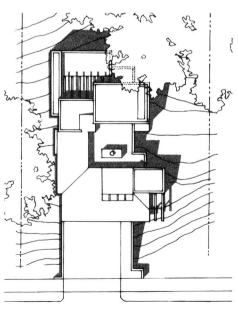

Roof plan

Planta de cubiertas

Dachgrundriss

First floor

Planta primera

Erster Stock

Second floor

Planta segunda

Zweiter Stock

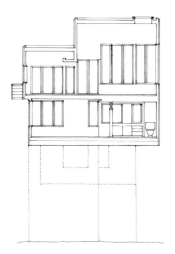

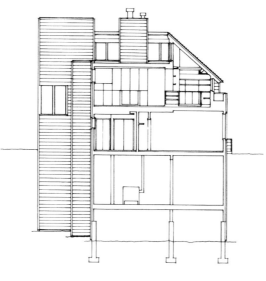

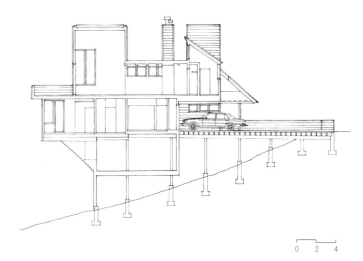

Transversal sections

Secciones transversales

Querschnitte

Longitudinal section

Sección longitudinal

Längsschnitt

Jonathan Levi Architects is an architecture and interior design firm. Their buildings and interior spaces support and reinforce the highest aspirations of their clients. Their source of inspiration for every project stems from a comprehensive study of the conditions surrounding the individual project, and the close collaboration of the client. A rigorous design method based on the exploration of different alternatives guides their response to each design challenge. This results in conceptual clarity and the responsible use of resources.

Jonathan Levi Architects es una firma de arquitectura y diseño interior que se encarga de que los edificios y los espacios interiores cumplan las máximas aspiraciones de sus clientes. En cada obra se toma como fuente de inspiración la estrecha colaboración con el cliente y una exhaustiva investigación de las condiciones que envuelven cada proyecto. La respuesta a cada situación viene dada por un riguroso método de diseño organizado a partir de la comprobación de diferentes alternativas. El resultado se traduce en una economía de medios y en una claridad conceptual.

Jonathan Levi Architects ist ein Architektur- und Innenarchitekturstudio, das Gebäude und Innenräume plant, die den Wünschen und Bedürfnissen ihrer Kunden so weit wie möglich gerecht werden. Bei jeder dieser Planungen ist die Inspirationsquelle die enge Zusammenarbeit mit dem Kunden und eine genaue Analyse der Bedingungen jedes einzelnen Bauvorhabens. Die Antwort auf jede Situation entsteht aus der strengen und organisierten Planung der Gestaltung nach Überprüfung mehrerer Alternativen. So entstehen Gebäude mit niedrigen Kosten und einem klaren Konzept.

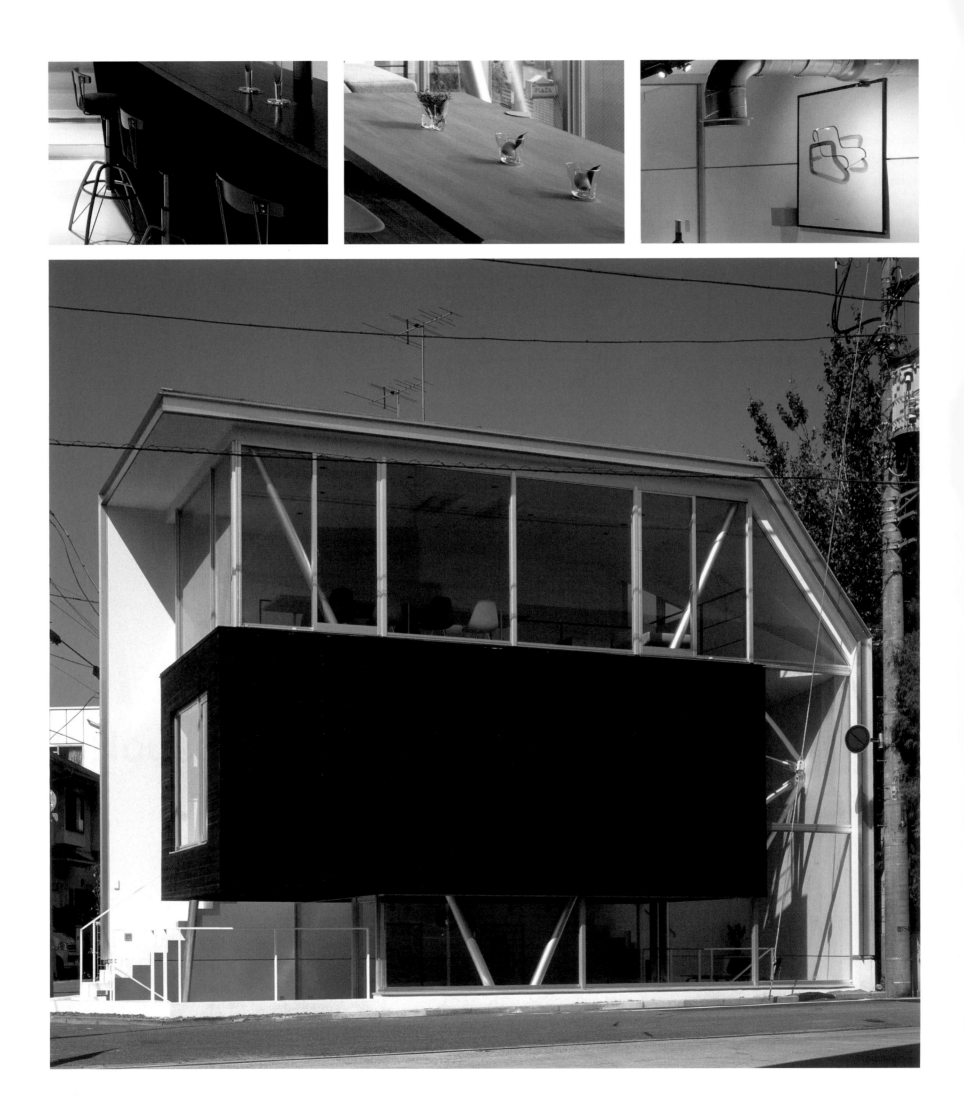

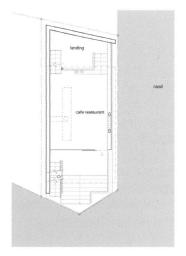

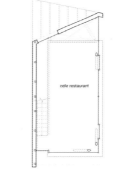

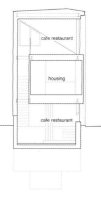

0   2   4

Ground floor

Planta baja

Erdgeschoss

First floor

Planta primera

Erster Stock

Second floor

Planta segunda

Zweiter Stock

Longitudinal section

Sección longitudinal

Längsschnitt

Transversal section

Sección transversal

Querschnitt

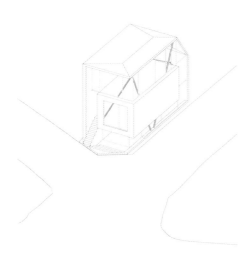

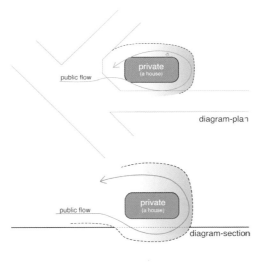

public flow

private
(a house)

diagram-plan

public flow

private
(a house)

diagram-section

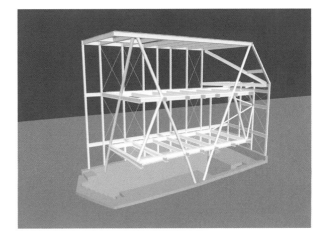

Axonometry

Axonometría

Axonometrie

Diagrams

Esquemas

Schema

1. What historical reference in particular inspires you when designing a residence?
   ¿Qué referente histórico en particular le sirve de fuente de inspiración a la hora de proyectar una vivienda?
   Welche historische Referenz dient Ihnen als Inspiration beim Entwurf eines Hauses?

2. What is the main factor taken into consideration when designing a residence?
   ¿Cuál es el principal factor determinante a la hora de diseñar una vivienda?
   Welche Rahmenbedingungen, bzw. Faktoren sind für Sie ausschlaggebend beim Konzipieren?

3. What room inside the home do you find most interesting to design?
   ¿Qué estancia de la vivienda encuentra usted más interesante para diseñar?
   Welchen Raum des Hauses finden Sie am spannendsten zu entwerfen?

4. What is your criteria for choosing materials and finishings in a particular room?
   ¿Cuál es su criterio a la hora de seleccionar los materiales y los acabados en esta estancia?
   Welche Kriterien wenden Sie bei der Entscheidung über Materialien und Oberflächen in diesem Raum an?

1. We explore flexible and transitive spatial condition in response to owners' needs. We try to understand the character of site as much as possible and then make it reflect on the positioning and composition of the residential space.

2. We don't design too much and try to leave the space or condition into which the owners can intervene spontaneously.

3. Communal space such as living, dinning and kitchen, because such space causes various interaction among the family.

4. We make an effort to transform the owners' requests into appropriate materials in a specific and precise manner.

1. Exploramos las condiciones de flexibilidad y transición del espacio en respuesta a las necesidades del propietario. Intentamos entender lo mejor posible las características del lugar para después reflejarlas en la situación y composición del espacio residencial.

2. No diseñamos demasiado, procuramos dejar el espacio en unas condiciones en las que los propietarios puedan intervenir espontáneamente.

3. Los espacios públicos, como la sala de estar, el comedor y la cocina, porque estos espacios promueven la interacción entre la familia.

4. Hacemos un esfuerzo para transformar las necesidades del propietario en los materiales adecuados de un modo preciso y específico.

1. Wir erforschen die Bedingungen der Flexibilität und des Übergangs des Raumes und versuchen damit, den Bedürfnissen des Eigentümers zu entsprechen. Wir versuchen, die Eigentümlichkeiten des Ortes so gut wie möglich zu verstehen, um sie dann in der Lage und Anordnung des Wohnhauses oder der Wohnung widerzuspiegeln.

2. Wir greifen zurückhaltend ein. Wir möchten den Raum so lassen, dass auch die Eigentümer spontane Eingriffe vornehmen können.

3. Die von allen genutzten Räume wie das Wohnzimmer, das Esszimmer und die Küche, da es die Räume sind, in denen das Familienleben stattfindet.

4. Wir versuchen, die geeigneten Materialien präzise und spezifisch für die Bedürfnisse des Kunden auszuwählen.

Tele-design was established with the purpose of incorporating two important tendencies of contemporary Japanese society into the vision and structure of the company. The first was the pursuit of new models of economic growth, and the second was the rapid development of telecommunications within the global economy. In this way design becomes a tool for exploration as well as a vehicle for the incorporation of the latest technologies. Tele-design consists of a multi-disciplinary team that has worked together since 1999. Its unique structure has caught the attention of clients, the press and international critics.

Tele-design se estableció con ánimo de incorporar dos tendencias significativas de la actual sociedad japonesa en la visión y estructura de la compañía. En primer lugar, la búsqueda de nuevos modelos tras el crecimiento económico y en segundo lugar, el rápido desarrollo de las telecomunicaciones en la economía global. De esta manera, el diseño se convierte en una herramienta para explorar y nutrirse de las últimas tecnologías. Por este motivo, tele-design está formado por un equipo pluridisciplinar que colabora junto desde 1999. Su particular estructura ha llamado la atención no sólo de clientes, sino de la prensa y la crítica internacional.

Tele-design wurde gegründet, um zwei wichtige Tendenzen der heutigen japanischen Gesellschaft in die Unternehmensstruktur zu integrieren. Diese Tendenzen sind die Suche nach neuen Modellen nach dem starken Wirtschaftswachstum und die schnelle Entwicklung der Telekommunikationen in der globalen Wirtschaft. So wurde das Design zu einem Werkzeug, um die neusten Technologien zu erforschen und sich von ihnen zu nähren. Tele-design arbeitet daher seit 1999 mit einem multidisziplinäres Team. Diese besondere Struktur erweckte viel Aufmerksamkeit seitens der Kunden und der internationalen Presse und Kritik.

Ground floor

Planta baja

Erdgeschoss

First floor

Planta primera

Erster Stock

Second floor

Planta segunda

Zweiter Stock

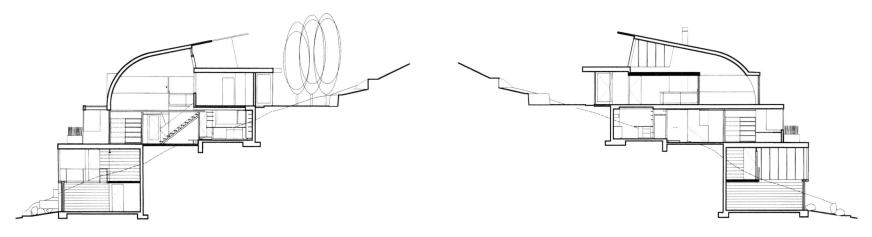

0   2   4

Sections

Secciones

Schnitte

1. What historical reference in particular inspires you when designing a residence?
¿Qué referente histórico en particular le sirve de fuente de inspiración a la hora de proyectar una vivienda?
Welche historische Referenz dient Ihnen als Inspiration beim Entwurf eines Hauses?

2. What is the main factor taken into consideration when designing a residence?
¿Cuál es el principal factor determinante a la hora de diseñar una vivienda?
Welche Rahmenbedingungen, bzw. Faktoren sind für Sie ausschlaggebend beim Konzipieren?

3. What room inside the home do you find most interesting to design?
¿Qué estancia de la vivienda encuentra usted más interesante para diseñar?
Welchen Raum des Hauses finden Sie am spannendsten zu entwerfen?

4. What is your criteria for choosing materials and finishings in a particular room?
¿Cuál es su criterio a la hora de seleccionar los materiales y os acabados en esta estancia?
Welche Kriterien wenden Sie bei der Entscheidung über Materialien und Oberflächen in diesem Raum an?

1. We look at the history of the context, for traces of what came before. We may find and build upon a salient part of that memory, not in a sentimental or representational way, but by an abstraction of or an enactment of it.

2. In our design, the choreography of the human experience precedes the genesis of form.

3. We find interstitial spaces, such as the residual plazas and paseos left from the figure of the buildings to be some of the most interesting places of an urbanscape.

4. We believe in the responsible use of resources, and in the expression of material and structure as an integral part of how the environment is made. Materials can be a kind of chronicle of the building's making; from the concrete foundation walls, the heavy steel structure, the light gauge steel skeleton, the flesh of the plastered walls to infill of the cabinetry and partitions.

1. Tenemos en cuenta la historia del entorno, buscando rastros de lo que hubo antes. Es posible que los encontremos y que la construcción parta de ese recuerdo, no de un modo sentimental o figurativo, sino mediante su abstracción o recreación.

2. En nuestro diseño, la coreografía de la experiencia humana precede a la génesis de la forma.

3. Los espacios, como las plazas y los paseos alejados de los edificios, nos resultan lugares de lo más interesante dentro del paisaje urbano.

4. Creemos en el uso responsable de los recursos y en la expresión del material y la estructura como parte integral de cómo está constituido el entorno. Los materiales pueden ser una especie de crónica de la edificación: desde los cimientos de hormigón, la pesada estructura de metal, el ligero esqueleto de acero hasta las paredes de yeso que albergan el mobiliario y las particiones.

1. Wir beachten stets die Geschichte des Kontexts. Es ist möglich, dass wir Spuren finden und dass der Bau von dieser Erinnerung ausgeht, aber nicht auf sentimentale oder figurative Weise, sondern durch die Abstraktion und Nachahmung der Vergangenheit.

2. In unseren Entwürfen geht der Choreographie der menschlichen Erfahrung die Entstehung der Form voraus.

3. Die Räume wie die Plätze und Gänge, die von den Formen der Gebäude getrennt sind, sind für uns die interessantesten Orte innerhalb der Stadtlandschaft.

4. Für uns ist der verantwortungsvolle Einsatz von Mitteln und die Ausdrucksfähigkeit des Materials und der Struktur als integraler Bestandteil unserer Umgebung von großer Bedeutung. Die Materialien können eine Art Chronik des Baus darstellen, angefangen bei dem Fundament aus Beton, der schweren Metallstruktur, dem leichten Stahlskelett bis hin zu den Gipswänden, in denen Möbel und die Unterteilungen untergebracht sind.

Fung + Blatt Architects, founded in 1990 by Alice Fung and Michael Rosner Blatt, is a firm with five people dedicated to designing residential, commercial, and community projects. Their background in structural design and art results in projects that maintain a balance among structure, architecture, and landscape. This multidisciplinary team believes that the group effort helps all the pieces of a project fit together. They are committed to using resources responsibly in a design that is adapted to the surroundings, that acknowledges the past, and that anticipates the changes in the future of each client.

Fung + Blatt Architects, fundada por Alice Fung y Michael Rosner Blatt en 1990, es una firma compuesta por cinco personas dedicadas al diseño de proyectos residenciales, comerciales y comunitarios. Su formación en diseño de estructuras y arte conduce su trabajo a un permanente análisis entre estructura, arquitectura y paisaje. El grupo cree en la suma de esfuerzos de un equipo pluridisciplinar que contribuye a que encajen todas las piezas de una obra. Está comprometido con el uso responsable de los recursos y en un diseño que se adapta al entorno, comprende el pasado y se anticipa a los cambios del futuro de cada cliente.

Fung + Blatt Architects wurde 1990 von Alice Fung und Michael Rosner Blatt gegründet. Es handelt sich um ein Unternehmen mit 5 Mitarbeitern, die sich dem Entwurf von Wohn-, Geschäfts- und Gemeinschaftsgebäuden widmen. Aufgrund ihrer Ausbildung im Bereich Architektur und Kunst ist die Grundlage ihrer Vorgehensweise eine permanente Analyse der Beziehung zwischen Struktur, Architektur und Landschaft. Sie glauben daran, dass durch die Summierung der Erfahrung und Arbeit eines multidisziplinären Teams ein Ergebnis erreicht wird, bei dem alle Teile in ein Gesamtwerk passen.

This house is located about 250 miles (400 kilometers) from São Paulo, Brazil, on a property with typically exuberant, tropical vegetation. The residence presents two sides that are clearly different yet complementary. From the outside it looks like an austere, contemporary building, but a glance at the exterior patio reveals a type of architecture with references that are clearly traditional. These two languages blend harmoniously, aided by the exterior landscape, which is always present in the home. The outside of the house is faced with mineira stone, which is typical of this region. The cement and natural stone floor, and the wood screens that let in the natural light, provide great warmth to the interior. The single-level home has an L-shape layout, and the peripheral wall on the other two sides defines the patio, which is faced by the bedrooms and the living room.

Du Plessis House

Marcio Kogan

São Paulo, Brazil, 2003
Photos © Arnaldo Pappalardo

La casa se encuentra a unos 400 kilómetros de São Paulo, Brasil, en un solar con exuberante vegetación, típicamente tropical. La casa presenta dos aspectos claramente diferenciados y al mismo tiempo complementarios. La apariencia exterior es la de un edificio austero y contemporáneo, mientras que si se echa un vistazo al patio exterior revela una arquitectura con claros referentes tradicionales. Estos dos lenguajes se superponen

Dieses Haus befindet sich 400 Kilometer von São Paulo, Brasilien, entfernt auf einem Grundstück mit einer üppigen, typisch tropischen Vegetation. Das Haus zeigt sich von zwei klar differenzierten Seiten, die sich gegenseitig ergänzen. Von außen handelt es sich um ein nüchternes und zeitgenössisches Haus, während ein Blick durch den Hof eine Architektur zeigt, die offensichtlich von der traditionellen Bauweise beeinflusst ist. Diese beiden Stile wer-

armónicamente apoyándose en el paisaje exterior, presente siempre en la vivienda. El volumen exterior está revestido de piedra mineira, material típico de esta región, y crea una caja que rodea un patio y en el cual se focaliza todo el área social de la casa. El pavimento de cemento y piedra natural así como las celosías de madera, tras las que se filtra la luz natural, otorgan una gran calidez a los interiores. La casa se desarrolla en una sola planta y se presenta un escuema en L, en donde las habitaciones y la sala de estar se abren al patio conformado por el muro perimetral.

den harmonisch mit einander kombiniert und durch eine Landschaft ergänzt, die auch im Haus immer präsent ist. Das Gebäude ist von außen mit Natursteinen aus Minas Gerais verkleidet, ein für diese Region typischer Stein, und formt einen Block, der einen Hof umgibt, zu dem hin die Wohn- und Aufenthaltsräume des Hauses liegen. Durch den Boden aus Zement und Naturstein und die Jalousien aus Holz, durch die sich das Tageslicht filtert, wirkt das Innere sehr warm. Das Haus besitzt nur ein Stockwerk und ist in L-Form angelegt. Die Schlafzimmer und das Wohnzimmer liegen zum Hof, der von einer Mauer umgeben wird.

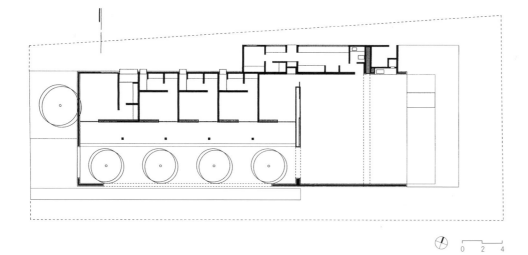

Ground floor

Planta baja

Erdgeschoss

Side elevation

Alzado lateral

Seitenaufriss

Elevations

Alzados

Aufrisse

Marcio Kogan graduated from the Mackenzie School of Architecture in 1976. Since that time he has received many awards for different architectural assignments. He has designed a variety of small-scale and large-scale projects, mainly in Sao Paulo, Brazil and the surrounding area. His architectural work is known for its strong, refined lines. Since 1974 he combines architecture projects with his passion for the cinema. He has created a great number of short films, and his first full-length movie was made in 1988.

Marcio Kogan se graduó en la Escuela de Arquitectura Mackenzie en 1976 y desde entonces ha recibido numerosos premios por varias de sus obras arquitectónicas. Ha diseñado una amplia variedad de proyectos de pequeña y gran escala, principalmente en São Paulo, Brasil, y sus alrededores. Su trabajo como arquitecto, en donde destaca una depurada y contundente línea de diseño, lo combina desde 1974 con su pasión por el cine, disciplina en la que ha realizado numerosos cortometrajes y un primer largo en 1988.

Marcio Kogan schloss sein Studium 1976 an der Mackenzie School of Architecture ab und ist seitdem mit zahlreichen Preisen für verschiedene seiner Bauten ausgezeichnet worden. Er hat eine ganze Reihe kleiner und großer Gebäude hauptsächlich in Sao Paulo, Brasilien, und Umgebung entworfen. Seine Arbeit als Architekt ist vor allem von der Klarheit und Überzeugungskraft seiner Entwürfe gekennzeichnet, die er seit 1974 mit seiner Leidenschaft für das Kino kombiniert. Er hat für eine ganze Reihe von Kurzfilmen und 1988 auch für einen Spielfilm Regie geführt.

1. What historical reference in particular inspires you when designing a residence?

¿Qué referente histórico en particular le sirve de fuente de inspiración a la hora de proyectar una vivienda?

Welche historische Referenz dient Ihnen als Inspiration beim Entwurf eines Hauses?

2. What is the main factor taken into consideration when designing a residence?

¿Cuál es el principal factor determinante a la hora de diseñar una vivienda?

Welche Rahmenbedingungen, bzw. Faktoren sind für Sie ausschlaggebend beim Konzipieren?

3. What room inside the home do you find most interesting to design?

¿Qué estancia de la vivienda encuentra usted más interesante para diseñar?

Welchen Raum des Hauses finden Sie am spannendsten zu entwerfen?

4. What is your criteria for choosing materials and finishings in a particular room?

¿Cuál es su criterio a la hora de seleccionar los materiales y los acabados en esta estancia?

Welche Kriterien wenden Sie bei der Entscheidung über Materialien und Oberflächen in diesem Raum an?

---

1. The architect works from memory. Not just based on history, but drawing selectively and critically from his or her knowledge of history. Therefore, all previous experience is reference material for projects. From this premise, as Quaroni said, history becomes a tool, knowledge of which is indispensable, but once you know it, it cannot be used without interpretation.

2. Architecture is a problem of proportion and balance. There is no single determinant factor but many, whose simultaneous consideration is essential. Good architecture is always complex and satisfies a myriad of functional, design, cultural requirements at the same time.

3. Every room is important and interesting from the standpoint of the house as a whole, as a setting for relationships among the family members, and between them and society.

4. There is no single, previously existing criterium, but criteria that depend on a multitude of factors.

---

1. El arquitecto proyecta desde la memoria. No sólo a partir de la historia, sino desde la elaboración crítica y selectiva del conocimiento histórico. Así pues, toda la experiencia previa es referencia proyectual.

2. La arquitectura es un problema de proporciones y equilibrios. No hay un factor determinante, sino muchos, cuya consideración simultánea es esencial. La buena arquitectura es siempre compleja y satisface a la vez multitud de requerimientos funcionales, programáticos, culturales, etcétera.

3. Desde la consideración de la vivienda como un conjunto, como un ámbito global de relación familiar y de esta con la sociedad, tocas las estancias son igualmente interesantes e importantes.

4. No hay criterio previo, sino criterios que dependen de multitud de factores.

---

1. Der Architekt entwirft aus dem Gedächtnis. Dabei beruft er sich nicht nur auf die Geschichte, sondern auch auf die kritische und selektive Ausarbeitung seiner historischen Kenntnisse. Deshalb ist jegliche Erfahrung eine Referenz für die Planung.

2. Die Architektur ist ein Problem von Proportionen und Gleichgewichten. Es gibt nicht einen entscheidenden Faktor, sondern viele. Es ist wichtig, sie alle gleichzeitig zu betrachten. Eine gute Architektur ist immer komplex und entspricht gleichzeitig einer Vielzahl von funktionellen, programmatischen, kulturellen, technischen und umweltbedingten Anforderungen.

3. Wenn man eine Wohnung als ein Ganzes betrachten, als eine globale Umgebung für die familiären Beziehungen und der Beziehungen der Familie zur Gesellschaft, dann sind alle Räume gleich interessant und wichtig.

4. Es gibt kein Kriterium, das schon vorher feststeht, sondern nur Kriterien, die von einer Vielzahl von Faktoren abhängen.

The architecture studio of Vicens + Ramos has been active since 1984. Ignacio Vicens and Hualde is a Professor of Planning in the School of Architecture in Madrid, where he is also the Assistant Director of Doctoral Research and Postgraduate Studies. José Antonio Ramos Abengózar is a Professor of Planning in the same school. The focus of the studio is a combination of professional activity and teaching, which leads to continuous research that feeds the design process. The firm has received numerous awards in Spain for a wide range of projects.

El estudio de arquitectura Vicens + Ramos desarrolla su actividad desde 1984. Ignacio Vicens y Hualde es catedrático de proyectos en la Escuela de Arquitectura de Madrid, en donde al mismo tiempo es subdirector de doctorado, investigación y posgrado. José Antonio Ramos Abengózar es profesor de proyectos en la misma escuela. Compatibilizar la actividad profesional con la enseñanza académica marca la trayectoria del estudio, orientada hacia una continua investigación que alimenta el proceso de diseño. La firma ha recibido numerosos premios en España por varias de sus obra.

Das Architekturbüro Vicens + Ramos besteht seit 1984. Ignacio Vicens y Hualde ist Professor im Bereich Planung an der Architekturschule von Madrid, an der er auch gleichzeitig stellvertretender Direktor für die Dissertationen, Forschung und die postgraduierten Studien ist. José Antonio Ramos Abengózar ist Professor im Bereich Planung an der gleichen Fachhochschule. Diese akademische Lehrtätigkeit prägt auch die Arbeit des Unternehmens, in dem die ständige Forschung die Grundlage für den Gestaltungsprozess bildet. Dem Unternehmen wurden zahlreiche spanische Preise für mehrere Gebäude verschiedener Art verliehen.

The design of this single-family home is based on the fact that today the city of Yokohama is considered one more suburb of the rapidly growing Tokyo metropolitan area. The property, despite being on a hill, has a strong urban feeling, yet it has no tendency towards a specific style. The design approach was based on a review of the conditions of the site and the creation of a series of functions related to each other and to the exterior. The L-shaped configuration allowed the creation of a versatile interior. The different terraces and spaces that face the patio, which resulted from the shape of the house, play off each other to create many scenarios and uses for each room. The extension of the interior spaces towards the outside terraces is emphasized by using the same materials and finishes in both. This approach also created a harmonious relationship between the interior environment and the general context of the neighborhood. From outside, on the other hand, the look proposed for the façade was one of enclosure and austerity to reflect the surrounding structures.

Double-L

Noriyuki Tajima / tele-design

Yokohama, Japan, 2002
Photos © Tatsuya Noaki

Debido al increíble crecimiento del área metropolitana de Tokio, la ciudad de Yokchama es actualmente considerada un barrio más de la ciudad. El proyecto para esta vivienda unifamiliar está basado en esta condición. La ubicación del solar, a pesar de encontrarse en una colina, presentaba un marcado carácter urbano sin ningún carácter en particular. La propuesta parte entonces de reconsiderar la condición del lugar y crear una secuencia

Aufgrund des unglaublich schnellen Wachstums des Stadtgebietes von Tokio kann man die Stadt Yokohama heute fast als einen weiteren Vorort von Tokio betrachten. Darauf basiert die Planung für dieses Einfamilienhaus. Es befindet sich auf einem Grundstück, das zwar auf einem Hügel gelegen ist, aber trotzdem einen sehr städtischen und relativ gewöhnlichen Charakter hat. Diese durch das Grundstück vorgegebenen Bedingungen beeinflussten die

de actividades relacionadas entre sí y con el exterior. La forma en L de la composición general permite crear un mundo interior en donde las diferentes terrazas y espacios que miran al patio logrado por esta forma se relacionan entre sí, creando una gran diversidad de situaciones y numerosas maneras de aprovechar cada estancia de la casa. La extensión de los espacios interiores hacia las terrazas exteriores se acentúan con el mismo criterio de acabados y materiales tanto en uno como en otro. Como resultado se logró crear todo un paisaje interior que se relaciona también con el contexto general del barrio. Desde la calle se propuso una fachada cerrada y austera que dialoga con el entorno construido.

Planung in der Weise, dass man versuchte, eine Reihe von miteinander und mit der Außenwelt verbundenen Elementen zu schaffen. Durch die Anlage einer L-Form entstand eine innere Welt, in der verschiedene Terrassen und Räume, die zum Hof liegen, miteinander in Beziehung stehen, so dass viele verschiedene Situationen und räumliche Möglichkeiten in dem Haus entstehen. Die Tatsache, dass die Innenräume auf die Außenterrassen hin ausgerichtet sind, wird noch durch die verwendeten Materialien in den Räumen und auf den Terrassen unterstrichen. So entstand eine innere Landschaft, die auch mit dem allgemeinen Kontext des Viertels in Verbindung steht. Von der Straße aus wirkt die Fassade geschlossen und nüchtern, jedoch gut in die bebaute Umgebung integriert.

Ground floor

Planta baja

Erdgeschoss

First floor

Planta primera

Erster Stock

Sections

Secciones

Schnitte

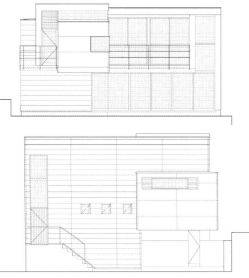

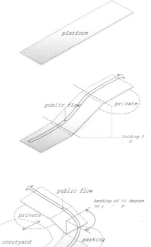

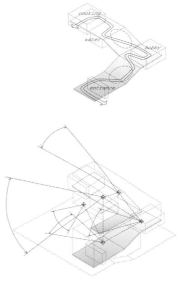

Elevations

Alzados

Aufrisse

Diagrams

Esquemas

Schema

1. What historical reference in particular inspires you when designing a residence?
¿Qué referente histórico en particular le sirve de fuente de inspiración a la hora de proyectar una vivienda?
Welche historische Referenz dient Ihnen als Inspiration beim Entwurf eines Hauses?

2. What is the main factor taken into consideration when designing a residence?
¿Cuál es el principal factor determinante a la hora de diseñar una vivienda?
Welche Rahmenbedingungen, bzw. Faktoren sind für Sie ausschlaggebend beim Konzipieren?

3. What room inside the home do you find most interesting to design?
¿Qué estancia de la vivienda encuentra usted más interesante para diseñar?
Welchen Raum des Hauses finden Sie am spannendsten zu entwerfen?

4. What is your criteria for choosing materials and finishings in a particular room?
¿Cuál es su criterio a la hora de seleccionar los materiales y los acabados en esta estancia?
Welche Kriterien wenden Sie bei der Entscheidung über Materialien und Oberflächen in diesem Raum an?

1. I don't have particular example but have some influences from historical Japanese residences and also 30's to 70's modern houses. Recently my interest moves to more 70's houses.

2. Three things in combination: Activities of the dwellers, natural environment such as light, wind and landscape, and urban context.

3. I am interested in more of erasing the separation of rooms and functions, trying to find flow of activities and living condition by connecting them, a house becomes more one room connected.

4. I do not choose materials which have too much strong expression, but I do rather use materials suitable to spatial compositions. Occasionally I use stronger material in order to emphasize its spatial quality. Mostly uses neutral material such as white walls.

1. No puedo nombrar a nadie en particular, pero sí tengo influencias de residencias japonesas históricas y también de casa modernas construidas entre los años 1930 y 1970. En la actualidad, mis intereses se mueven más cerca de las casa de la década de los setenta.

2. Tres factores combinados: las actividades de los residentes, el entorno natural (la luz, el viento, el paisaje) y el contexto urbano.

3. Estoy interesado en eliminar las separaciones de espacios y funciones y encontrar un flujo de actividades y condiciones de vida con la conexión de las estancias, de modo que la casa se convierte en una gran habitación interconectada.

4. No elijo materiales que tengan una expresión demasiado marcada, sino materiales que permitan crear combinaciones espaciales. Ocasionalmente uso materiales más fuertes con el fin de acentuar las cualidades del espacio. En la mayoría de los casos utilizo materiales neutros, como las paredes blancas.

1. Ich kann niemanden im Besonderen erwähnen, aber ich bin beeinflusst von den historischen japanischen Häusern, und auch von den modernen Häusern, die zwischen den Dreißiger- und Siebzigerjahren gebaut wurden. Im Augenblick interessiere ich mich mehr für die Häuser der Siebzigerjahre

2. Drei kombinierte Faktoren, die Aktivitäten der Bewohner, die natürliche Umgebung (Licht, Wind, Landschaft) und der städtische Kontext.

3. Ich versuche, die Trennung zwischen Räumen und Funktionen aufzuheben, und so ein Fließen der Aktivitäten und Lebensbedingungen zu erreichen, indem ich die Räume miteinander verbinde. So wird aus dem Haus ein großer, verbundener Raum.

4. Ich entscheide mich nicht für Materialien, die einen zu starken Ausdruck haben, sondern für Materialien, die sich auf besondere Art kombinieren lassen. Manchmal benutze ich starke Materialien, um eine Eigentümlichkeit des Raumes zu unterstreichen. Meist setze ich neutrale Materialien wie weiße Wände ein.

Tele-design was established with the purpose of incorporating two important tendencies of contemporary Japanese society into the vision and structure of the company. The first was the pursuit of new models of economic growth, and the second was the rapid development of telecommunications within the global economy. In this way design becomes a tool for exploration as well as a vehicle for the incorporation of the latest technologies. Tele-design consists of a multi-disciplinary team that has worked together since 1999. Its unique structure has caught the attention of clients, the press and international critics.

Tele-design se estableció con ánimo de incorporar dos tendencias significativas de la actual sociedad japonesa en la visión y estructura de la compañía. En primer lugar, la búsqueda de nuevos modelos tras el crecimiento económico y en segundo lugar, el rápido desarrollo de las telecomunicaciones en la economía global. De esta manera, el diseño se convierte en una herramienta para explorar y nutrirse de las últimas tecnologías. Por este motivo, tele-design está formado por un equipo pluridisciplinar que colabora junto desde 1999. Su particular estructura ha llamado la atención no sólo de clientes, sino de la prensa y la crítica internacional.

Tele-design wurde gegründet, um zwei wichtige Tendenzen der heutigen japanischen Gesellschaft in die Unternehmensstruktur zu integrieren. Diese Tendenzen sind die Suche nach neuen Modellen nach dem starken Wirtschaftswachstum und die schnelle Entwicklung der Telekommunikationen in der globalen Wirtschaft. So wurde das Design zu einem Werkzeug, um die neusten Technologien zu erforschen und sich von ihnen zu nähren. Tele-design arbeitet daher seit 1999 mit einem multidisziplinären Team. Diese besondere Struktur erweckte viel Aufmerksamkeit seitens der Kunden und der internationalen Presse und Kritik.

ATTICS
ÁTICOS / DACHWOHNUNGEN

Phillipps / Skaife Residence

Abbot Kinney Lofts

Brooklyn Loft

Vertical Loft

House in Kuessnacht

Shoreditch Conversion

Residence in Gracia

Motoazabu Housing Complex

Rooftop

Ray 1

Bay Cities Lofts: Phase II

One of the main interests of this architect, which is seen in all his projects, is the manipulation of light as a design element. His interest is not only in illuminating spaces, but also in using the light as a medium for imprinting a specific character on each area of the project. In this case the approach is complemented by the personalities of the clients, two movie producers who are seduced by bright and strong colors. The design had to resolve two residential scenarios that could function independently within the same long and narrow, two-level unit. To make up for the lack of light in this layout, typical of New York, the architect took advantage of the fact that the unit was on the top floor of the building to create a skylight that illuminates all the central part of the residence. The existing walls on the top floor, where the living and eating areas are located, were removed to create an open space that enhances the feeling of space and light.

Phillipps / Skaife Residence

Alden Maddry Architect

New York, NY, USA, 2002
Photos © Jordi Miralles

Una de las principales inquietudes en la trayectoria profesional de este arquitecto es la utilización de la luz como herramienta de diseño. Su interés radica no sólo en iluminar los espacios, sino en aprovechar la iluminación como medio para imprimir un rasgo específico a cada ámbito del proyecto. En el caso de este proyecto, se complementa con el carácter de sus clientes, una pareja de productores cinematográfcos, a quienes les seduce los

Dieser Architekt hat sich während seiner ganzen Laufbahn intensiv mit dem Licht als Gestaltungselement auseinandergesetzt. Dabei geht es nicht einfach nur darum, die Räume zu beleuchten, sondern die Beleuchtung als ein Mittel zu benutzen, um jedem Bereich eines Gebäudes einen besonderen Charakter zu verleihen. Im Falle dieses Bauwerkes wird diese Vorbedingung noch durch den Charakter der Kunden

colores intensos y brillantes. El diseño debía resolver dos programas de vivienda que funcionaran independientemente dentro de una misma unidad compuesta de dos plantas prolongadas. Para contrarrestar la falta de luz que generalmente hay en este tipo de configuración típica en Nueva York, se aprovechó que el volumen está situado en la última planta del edificio para crear una claraboya central que iluminara toda la parte central de la vivienda. La planta superior, en donde se ubican las zonas de estar y comedor, se liberaron de paredes existentes y se logró un espacio abierto en el que se acentúa aún más la sensación de amplitud y luminosidad.

ergänzt. Es handelt sich um ein Paar, das Kinofilme produziert und sich gerne von starken und glänzenden Farben verführen lässt. Durch die Gestaltung sollten zwei unabhängige Wohnbereiche innerhalb einer Einheit von zwei langen und engen Stockwerken untergebracht werden. Um den Lichtmangel auszugleichen, der normalerweise bei einer solchen, für New York typischen Gebäudeform herrscht, wurde die Tatsache ausgenutzt, dass die Räume sich im obersten Stockwerk des Gebäudes befinden und es wurde ein zentrales Dachfenster eingebaut, durch das Licht für den gesamten, mittleren Teil der Wohnung fällt. Im oberen Stockwerk, wo sich die Wohn- und Speisezimmer befinden, beseitigte man alle Wände, um einen offenen, weit und hell wirkenden Raum zu schaffen.

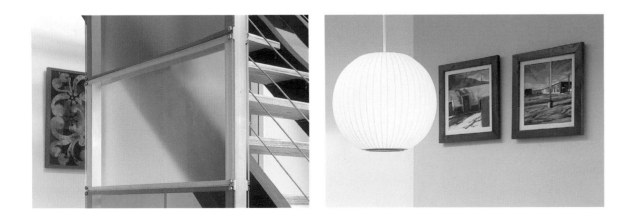

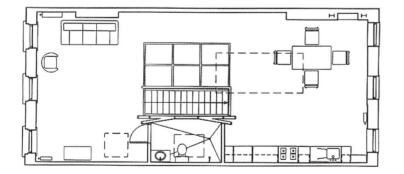

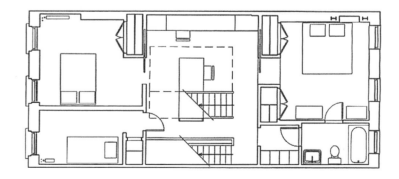

Ground floor

Planta baja

Erdgeschoss

First floor

Planta primera

Erster Stock

0   1   2

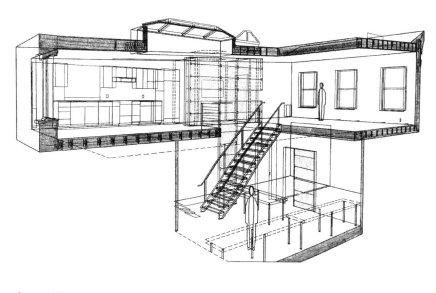

Axonometry

Axonometría

Axonometrie

1. What historical reference in particular inspires you when designing a residence?
   ¿Qué referente histórico en particular le sirve de fuente de inspiración a la hora de proyectar una vivienda?
   Welche historische Referenz dient Ihnen als Inspiration beim Entwurf eines Hauses?

2. What is the main factor taken into consideration when designing a residence?
   ¿Cuál es el principal factor determinante a la hora de diseñar una vivienda?
   Welche Rahmenbedingungen, bzw. Faktoren sind für Sie ausschlaggebend beim Konzipieren?

3. What room inside the home do you find most interesting to design?
   ¿Qué estancia de la vivienda encuentra usted más interesante para diseñar?
   Welchen Raum des Hauses finden Sie am spannendsten zu entwerfen?

4. What is your criteria for choosing materials and finishings in a particular room?
   ¿Cuál es su criterio a la hora de seleccionar los materiales y los acabados en esta estancia?
   Welche Kriterien wenden Sie bei der Entscheidung über Materialien und Oberflächen in diesem Raum an?

---

1. I draw inspiration from masterful individual houses and living spaces that range from the Maison de Verre in Paris to the Katsura Imperial Villa in Kyoto. But I have also drawn many ideas for my work from relatively unknown unpublished vernacular work from across the world.

2. How can I create spaces that will inspire my clients and enhance their experience of living.

3. There is not one particular room type that I find is consistently the most interesting to design. In fact the design of the interstitial spaces and connections between rooms can often be more interesting and add more to the design of the home than the composition of the individual rooms.

4. First I determine what function(s) the surface I am choosing will have. And by "function" I am not just talking about utilitarian concerns. Given these criteria I search for a possible material that can meet these requirements.

---

1. Encuentro inspiración en varios ejemplos famosos de proyectos de vivienda, desde la Maison de Verre en París hasta la Villa Imperial Katsura en Kioto. Pero también he aplicado muchas ideas en mi trabajo tomadas de obras vernaculares, desconocidas y poco publicadas alrededor del mundo.

2. Cómo puedo crear espacios que servirán de inspiración a mis clientes y realzar su experiencia de habitabilidad.

3. No hay una tipo de habitación en concreto que encuentre más interesante para diseñar. De hecho, el diseño de los espacios intersticiales y las conexiones entre habitaciones pueden ser más interesantes y aportar más al diseño de la casa que la composición de habitaciones individuales.

4. Primero determino qué función, y no solamente en términos utilitarios, tendrá la superficie que estoy eligiendo y con este criterio definido busco posibles materiales que puedan sustituir estas necesidades.

---

1. Mich inspirieren verschiedene Beispiele berühmter Planungen für Wohnhäuser, angefangen bei dem Maison de Verre in Paris bis zur Kaiserstadt Katsura in Kyoto. Ich habe aber auch viele Ideen in meinen Arbeiten umgesetzt, die aus volkstümlichen, architektonischen Werken stammen, und die weltweit relativ unbekannt sind und selten veröffentlicht wurden.

2. Wie kann ich Räume schaffen, die meine Kunden inspirieren und ihre Erfahrung im Wohnen betonen.

3. Es gibt keinen besonderen Typ Raum, den ich interessanter als andere finde. Tatsächlich kann die Gestaltung von Zwischenräumen und Verbindungen zwischen den verschiedenen Zimmern interessanter sein und mehr zum Design eines Hauses beitragen als die Gestaltung der individuellen Räume.

4. Zunächst bestimme ich die Funktion, nicht nur im Bezug auf die Benutzung, und sie wird die Fläche einnehmen, die ich wähle. Nachdem dieses Kriterium definiert wurde, wähle ich die möglichen Materialien für diese Bestimmung.

Alden Maddry Architect was founded in the spring of 1996. The firm specializes in cultural and residential designs, and projects related to art, in New York City and the surrounding area. Maddry is especially interested in the construction details and depends on the talent of expert workers and artisans of the region to carry out their projects. They have used alternative energy sources, — solar and geothermal — in many of their past projects.

Alden Maddry Architect fue fundada en primavera de 1996. La firma está especializada en diseños culturales y residenciales y en proyectos relacionados con el arte desarrollados en la ciudad de Nueva York y sus alrededores. Maddry está especialmente interesado en los procesos de construcción y se apoya en el talento de trabajadores y en artesanos expertos de la región para conformar sus proyectos. Fuentes de energía alternativa, como la energía solar o la geotermal, han sido utilizadas en proyectos pasados.

Alden Maddry Architect wurde im Frühjahr 1996 gegründet. Das Unternehmen ist auf Projekte in den Bereichen Kunst, Kultur und Stadtwohnungen in New York und Umgebung spezialisiert. Bei Maddry interessiert man sich besonders für die Bauprozesse; und die Arbeiten werden in Zusammenarbeit mit begabten Arbeitern und Handwerkern aus der Region durchgeführt. In vielen, bereits von Maddry errichteten Gebäuden wurde alternative Energiequellen wie Solarenergie oder Erdwärme benutzt.

The Abbot Kinney neighborhood in Venice, California, is rapidly becoming an artist's district. A growing number of designers, multimedia firms, and artists choose this neighborhood, which is turning into a lively and diverse community. These professionals are not only looking for a section of the city that identifies with their way of life, but also for interior spaces that adapt to their requirements. They are searching for more casual, informal, and flexible environments that allow them to live and work in the same space. This project consists of a typical adaptation of the traditional artist's loft, with large, open spaces that can be used for living or working, as required. The plan includes three different adjacent lofts that share the same structure, materials, and color palette, giving it the appearance of a compact building. These characteristics allow the creation of a continuous façade and a commercial row facing the street. All the units are separated by patios and are equipped with balconies, terraces, and glassed-in areas.

Abbot Kinney Lofts

Mark Mack Architects

Venice, CA, USA, 2001
Photos © Undine Pröhl

El barrio de Abbot Kinney, en Venice, California, se está convirtiendo rápidamente en un distrito de artistas. Cada año crece el número de diseñadores, firmas multimedias y artistas que escogen este sector para emplazar sus estudios y crear una comunidad diversa y vital. Esta nueva cultura de profesionales no sólo busca un sector de la ciudad que se identifique con su modo de vida, sino también espacios interiores que se adapten a sus necesi-

Abbot Kinney in Venice, Kalifornien, entwickelt sich zur Zeit zunehmend zu einem Künstlerviertel. Jedes Jahr gibt es mehr Designer, Multimedia-Unternehmen und Künstler, die sich dieses Viertel für ihre Studios aussuchen, wodurch eine vielseitige und lebendige Gemeinschaft entstanden ist. Diese Menschen in kreativen Berufen suchen nicht nur ein Viertel in der Stadt, das ihrem Lebensstil zusagt, sondern auch Räume, die ihren

dades. Entornos más casuales, informales, flexibles, que permitan vivir y trabajar en una misma superficie, son las principales características de esta búsqueda. Este proyecto consiste en una adaptación tipológica del tradicional loft de artistas en el que se crea espacios amplios y abiertos que permiten ser usados como vivienda o zona de trabajo según las necesidades. El conjunto está compuesto por tres diferentes lofts adyacentes que comparten misma estructura, materiales y paleta de colores, de esta manera toma la apariencia de una unidad. Esto contribuye a crear una fachada continua y un paseo comercial orientado a la calle. mientras que cada uno de los volúmenes está separado por patios y disfruta de zonas acristaladas, balcones y terrazas.

Bedürfnissen entsprechen. Weniger strenge, flexible und moderne Räume, in denen man gleichzeitig leben und arbeiten kann, werden besonders gesucht. Dieses Projekt besteht in einer typischen Gestaltung eines traditionellen Künstler-Loftes, in dem weite und offene Räume geschaffen werden, die man sowohl zum Wohnen als auch zum Arbeiten benutzen kann. Das Gebäude beherbergt drei benachbarte Lofts, die die gleiche Struktur, Materialien und Farbpalette teilen, so dass ein zusammenhängendes Ganzes entsteht. So konnte auch eine durchgehende Fassade und ein kommerziell genutzter Weg zur Straße hin geschaffen werden, während alle Lofts durch Höfe getrennt sind und ihre eigenen verglasten Bereiche, Balkone und Terrassen haben.

Ground floor

Planta baja

Erdgeschoss

First floor

Planta primera

Erster Stock

Second floor

Planta segunda

Zweiter Stock

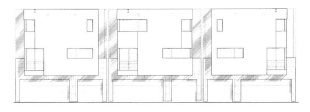

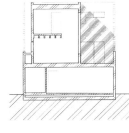

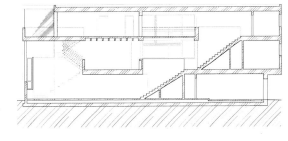

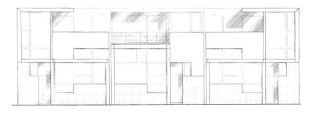

0 2 4

Elevations

Alzados

Aufrisse

Sections

Secciones

Schnitte

Mark Mack, along with his former partner Andrew Batey, earned his reputation as an architect in California mainly for his single-family home and villa designs in the early 1980's. He established his own office in San Francisco in 1984 and then moved to Venice, California in 1993. His approach to design is influenced by his academic work and restless curiosity. He was a professor in the School of Architecture at the University of California, Los Angeles. He was also a cofounder of Archetype Magazine and has contributed numerous articles to different magazines.

Mark Mack, junto a su antiguo socio Andrew Batey, se ha ganado su reputación como arquitecto en California principalmente por el diseño de villas y casas unifamiliares al inicio de la década de 1980. Estableció su propia oficina en San Francisco en 1984 y posteriormente se desplazó a Venice, California, en 1993. Su acercamiento al diseño está influenciado por sus inquietudes y su trabajo académico. Fue profesor de la Escuela de Arquitectura en la Universidad de California, Los Ángeles; asimismo fue cofundador de la revista Archetype Magazine y colaborador en numerosos artículos en diversas publicaciones.

Mark Mack begann seine Karriere Anfang der Achtzigerjahre mit der Planung von Einfamilienhäusern und Villen in Kalifornien zusammen mit seinem ehemaligen Teilhaber Andrew Batey. 1984 gründete er in San Francisco sein eigenes Unternehmen, das er 1993 nach Venice, Kalifornien, verlegte. Seine Interessen und seine akademische Arbeit beeinflussen stark seinen Gestaltungsstil. Er war Professor am Fachbereich Architektur der Universität von Kalifornien in Los Angeles. Ebenso war er Mitbegründer der Zeitschrift Archetype Magazine, in der er zahlreiche Artikel veröffentlicht hat.

This project is located in a space that was originally occupied by a lighting factory in an industrial neighborhood of the borough of Brooklyn, New York. The project had to fulfill the expectations of the clients, two artists from Brazil who wanted a loft-style space that would provide various settings for living as well as for working. A translucent, retractable wall defines the different areas in the lower level and adds character to the space. The natural light from a skylight flows through the translucent wall to illuminate the interior of the loft's living area. A dramatic metal stairway, light and equally transparent, connects the lower level with the top level where the bedrooms and an outdoor terrace are found. At the same time the stairway serves as an esthetic reference to the industrial nature of the building's past. The original façade, consisting of a garage door, and the new aluminum and wood features emphasize the contrast between the warm and organic interior and the heavy and metallic materials of the exterior.

Brooklyn Loft

Basil Walter Architects

New York, NY, USA, 2002
Photos © Bilyana Dimitrova

El proyecto se ubica en un terreno que fue originalmente ocupado por una fábrica de iluminación en el barrio industrial del distrito de Brooklyn, en Nueva York. El proyecto debía cumplir las expectativas de los clientes, una pareja brasileña de artistas, que querían disponer de un espacio tipo loft que evocara situaciones diversas tanto para vivir como para trabajar. Una pared retráctil y translúcida define y otorga carácter a las diferentes zonas en

Dieses Gebäude befindet sich auf einem Grundstück im Industrieviertel von Brooklyn, New York, auf dem einst eine Lampenfabrik stand. Die Kunden, ein brasilianisches Künstlerpaar, wünschten sich eine Art Loft, in dem man sowohl wohnen als auch arbeiten kann. Eine einziehbare und lichtdurchlässige Wand definiert und bereichert die verschiedenen Zonen im Erdgeschoss. Das Tageslicht dringt über ein Dachfenster ein und filtert sich durch die

la planta baja del espacio. La luz natural que desciende de la claraboya se filtra por la pared translúcida e ilumina el interior de la zona de la vivienda. Una dramática escalera metálica, ligera y transparente, conecta la planta baja con el nivel superior en donde se ubican las habitaciones y una terraza exterior. La escalera, por otra parte, sirve como recuerdo estético de la antigua naturaleza industrial del edificio en el pasado. La fachada original, compuesta por una puerta de garaje, y la nueva terraza de aluminio y madera acentúan el contraste entre el cálido interior orgánico y los detalles metálicos y pesados del exterior.

lichtdurchlässige Wand, so dass auch das Innere des Wohnbereiches beleuchtet wird. Eine dramatisch wirkende, leichte und ebenfalls transparente Metalltreppe verbindet das Erdgeschoss mit dem Obergeschoss, in dem sich die Schlafzimmer und die Terrasse im Freien befinden. Die Treppe dient auch als ästhetische Anspielung auf die industrielle Vergangenheit des Gebäudes. Die Originalfassade, die aus einer Garagentür besteht, und die neue Terrasse aus Aluminium und Holz unterstreichen den deutlich erkennbaren Unterschied zwischen den warm und organisch wirkenden Materialien im Inneren und den schweren Details aus Metall außen.

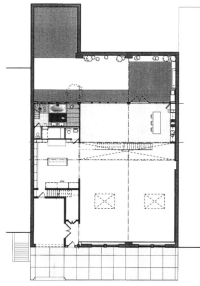

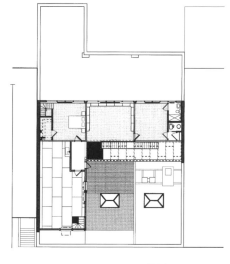

Ground floor

Planta baja

Erdgeschoss

First floor

Planta primera

Erster Stock

0   2   4

1. What historical reference in particular inspires you when designing a residence?

¿Qué referente histórico en particular le sirve de fuente de inspiración a la hora de proyectar una vivienda?

Welche historische Referenz dient Ihnen als Inspiration beim Entwurf eines Hauses?

2. What is the main factor taken into consideration when designing a residence?

¿Cuál es el principal factor determinante a la hora de diseñar una vivienda?

Welche Rahmenbedingungen, bzw. Faktoren sind für Sie ausschlaggebend beim Konzipieren?

3. What room inside the home do you find most interesting to design?

¿Qué estancia de la vivienda encuentra usted más interesante para diseñar?

Welchen Raum des Hauses finden Sie am spannendsten zu entwerfen?

4. What is your criteria for choosing materials and finishings in a particular room?

¿Cuál es su criterio a la hora de seleccionar los materiales y los acabados en esta estancia?

Welche Kriterien wenden Sie bei der Entscheidung über Materialien und Oberflächen in diesem Raum an?

---

1. It is the reference to historical methods rather than any direct period references which find their way most consistently into our work. A study of historical systems of design and construction creates a process that integrates time tested methods with free-thinking inventiveness.

2. What is most important is keeping the brightest torch shining firmly on those qualities of the house that make it beautiful, functional and economical and not getting sidetracked during the process. This requires continual reserves of energy and patience.

3. It is the connections between the various rooms or spaces in a home that pose the most challenging design issues.

4. The space itself must be the dominant image. Instances of local color or pattern must complement the effect of the space itself, and not the other way around.

---

1. En nuestro trabajo utilizamos habitualmente referencias a métodos históricos más que a periodos concretos. Un estudio de sistemas históricos de diseño y construcción constituye un proceso que integra métodos probados en una inventiva escéptica.

2. Lo más importante es realzar las cualidades que hacen que una vivienda sea bella, funcional y económica, sin que caigan en el olvido durante el proceso. Esto requiere continuas reservas de energía y paciencia.

3. Los elementos que presentan el mayor desafío durante el proceso de diseño son las conexiones entre las diferentes habitaciones o áreas.

4. El espacio en sí mismo debe ser la imagen dominante. Los elementos puntuales de color o forma deben complementar el efecto del espacio, no al revés.

---

1. Bei unserer Arbeit benutzen wir normalerweise eher Referenzen auf historische Methoden als auf konkrete Epochen der Zeitgeschichte. Eine Studie der historischen Systeme bei der Gestaltung und beim Bau stellt einen Prozess dar, der erprobte Methoden in eine skeptische Erfindungsgabe integriert.

2. Es ist wichtig, die Eigenschaften zu betonen, die dafür sorgen, dass ein Haus oder eine Wohnung schön, funktionell und ökonomisch werden. Diese Eigenschaften darf man während des Gesamtprozesses nicht vergessen, und dazu braucht man ständige Energie und Geduldsreserven.

3. Die Elemente, die die größte Herausforderung beim Planungsprozess darstellen, sind die Verbindungen zwischen den verschiedenen Räumen und Bereichen.

4. Der Raum selbst sollte das dominierende Bild sein. Einzelne, farbige Elemente oder Formen sollten die Wirkung des Raumes ergänzen, und nicht umgekehrt.

Basil Walter Architects was officially launched in 2001 after practicing for twelve years as Sweeny Walter Architects, founded in 1998. Today it is an organization of 13 architects and designers led by Basil Walter and his associate Brenda Bello. Basil Walter Architects and his previous firm were responsible for a variety of projects ranging from private residences to design offices and event planning. The firm, based in New York City, has ample experience in designing emblematic buildings as well as in renovating the interiors of many apartments in historic buildings.

Basil Walter Architects comenzó oficialmente en el año 2001 después de 12 años de trabajo como Sweeny Walter Architects, fundada en 1998. En la actualidad, es una organización de 13 arquitectos y diseñadores liderados por Basil Walter y su socia Brenda Bello. Basil Walter Architects y su firma predecesora han sido responsables del diseño de una amplia variedad de proyectos que se extienden desde viviendas privadas hasta oficinas de diseño o montaje de eventos. La firma, con sede en Nueva York, tiene amplia experiencia en el diseño de edificios emblemáticos así como en la reforma de apartamentos en edificios históricos.

Basil Walter Architects wurde offiziell 2001 gegründet, nachdem bereits 12 Jahre unter dem Namen Sweeny Walter Architects, gegründet 1989, gearbeitet wurde. Heute arbeiten 13 freie Architekten und Innenarchitekten für Basil Walter und seine Gesellschafterin Brenda Bello. Basil Walter Architects und die Vorgängerfirma haben bereits sehr verschiedene Planungen durchgeführt, Privatwohnungen, edle Büroräume und Bauten für Veranstaltungen. In New York blickt man auf eine lange Erfahrung in der Planung von emblematischen Gebäuden und Innenrenovierung von Wohnungen in historischen Gebäuden zurück.

This project is located in an old industrial space in the 11th District in Paris. It is not a typical industrial building with a horizontal, open, and fluid space, but one that is vertical and sturdy, made of wood and metal covered with rustic walls of exposed brick. The interior was opened up by removing all the dividing walls to create a naturally illuminated space of generous proportions. The structural and architectural elements that define and create the character of the interior space were preserved. The vertical aspect of the building offered the opportunity to create a design that exceeded the limits of a traditional loft. The project attempted to create a vertical sequence that highlight the dynamism of the design. Making an analogy to a movie script, the design lays out a sequence between what is seen, what is not seen, and what one hopes to see, all integrated into a common setting. The building was left completely intact, and certain aspects of the design took the form of solid spaces with opaque and translucent qualities. These volumes become anecdotes within the sequence.

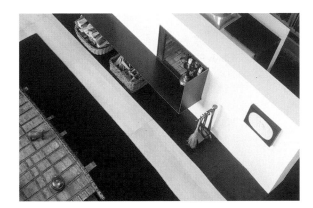

Vertical Loft

Insite Architecture Design

Paris, France, 2003
Photos © Georges Fessy

El proyecto se ubica en un antiguo terreno industrial en el distrito 11 de París. No se trata de la típica nave industrial en donde se plantearía un esquema en horizontal, abierto y fluido, sino que consiste en una estructura robusta de madera y metal que presenta una composición en vertical envuelta por una pared de aspecto rústico de ladrillo a la vista. Se liberó el espacio interior, eliminando todas las divisiones interiores, para obtener un espacio diáfano

Dieses Loft befindet sich in einem ehemaligen Industriegebäude im 11. Arrondissement von Paris. Es handelt sich nicht um das typische Fabrikgebäude mit einem horizontalen, offenen und fließenden Aufbau, sondern um eine robuste Struktur aus Holz und Metall, die sich vertikal aufbaut und von einer rustikalen Wand aus unverputztem Ziegelstein umgeben ist. Die Innenräume wurden erweitert, indem man alle Zwischenwände abriss.

y de generosas proporciones. Se mantuvieron y rescataron los elementos estructurales y arquitectónicos que definen y subrayan el carácter del espacio interior. La naturaleza vertical del volumen ofrecía una oportunidad para crear un proyecto que fuera más allá de los límites del loft tradicional. El proyecto debía crear una secuencia en vertical que revelara el dinamismo del programa. A semejanza de un guión cinematográfico, el diseño plantea una secuencia entre lo que se ve, lo que no se ve y lo que se espera ver relacionado por un escenario común. El volumen se respetó en su totalidad y ciertos aspectos del programa se materializaron en forma de piezas sólidas de cualidades translúcidas u opacas. Estos volúmenes se convierten en anécdotas dentro de la secuencia.

So erreichte man großzügige Proportionen und ließ das Tageslicht in die Räume eindringen. Die strukturellen und architektonischen Elemente, die die Räume prägen, wurden beibehalten und wieder hergestellt. Die vertikale Gliederung des Gebäudes machte es möglich, Räumlichkeiten zu schaffen, in denen mehr Kreativität als in einer traditionellen Fabriketage möglich war. Es wurde eine vertikale Sequenz geschaffen, die die Dynamik der Planung zeigte. Analog zu dem Drehbuch eines Films wird mit der Gestaltung eine Sequenz vorgeschlagen, eine Sequenz zwischen dem, was man sieht, dem was man nicht sieht und dem, was man zu sehen erwartet, all das am gleichen Schauplatz. Die Formen wurden absolut respektiert und bestimmte Aspekte der Gestaltung zeigten sich in festen Elementen, die doch lichtdurchlässig oder opak sind. Diese Formen werden zu Anekdoten innerhalb einer Sequenz.

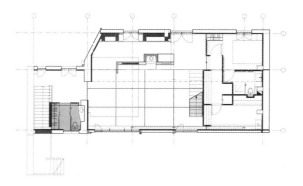

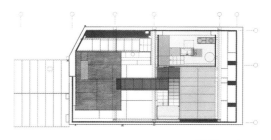

0   2   4

Ground floor

Planta baja

Erdgeschoss

First floor

Planta primera

Erster Stock

Second floor

Planta segunda

Zweiter Stock

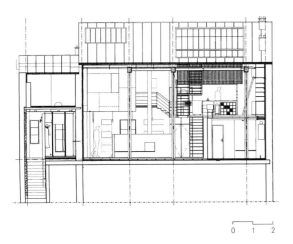

0 1 2

Longitudinal section

Sección longitudinal

Längsschnitt

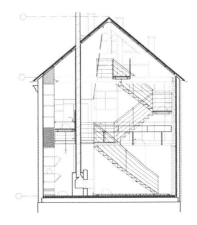

Transversal section

Sección transversal

Querschnitt

1. What historical reference in particular inspires you when designing a residence?
   ¿Qué referente histórico en particular le sirve de fuente de inspiración a la hora de proyectar una vivienda?
   Welche historische Referenz dient Ihnen als Inspiration beim Entwurf eines Hauses?

2. What is the main factor taken into consideration when designing a residence?
   ¿Cuál es el principal factor determinante a la hora de diseñar una vivienda?
   Welche Rahmenbedingungen, bzw. Faktoren sind für Sie ausschlaggebend beim Konzipieren?

3. What room inside the home do you find most interesting to design?
   ¿Qué estancia de la vivienda encuentra usted más interesante para diseñar?
   Welchen Raum des Hauses finden Sie am spannendsten zu entwerfen?

4. What is your criteria for choosing materials and finishings in a particular room?
   ¿Cuál es su criterio a la hora de seleccionar los materiales y los acabados en esta estancia?
   Welche Kriterien wenden Sie bei der Entscheidung über Materialien und Oberflächen in diesem Raum an?

1. We look at the social and built history of the region. We dissect these events and the periods that seem most pertinent to the project at hand and us.

2. There are several factors that cannot be left to the side. The history of the site, the program, which is most often stipulated by the client, and probably the most important factor is the intrinsic value-system of the client and how this system matches your own.

3. All. A house is not comprised of a series of discreet design instances, but rather is a puzzle of its different parts, so one 'room' cannot be more interesting than the other.

4. The site and the type of project dictate the materials. Then there are of course the individual economics of a project that play an important role when the final decision making takes place.

1. Nos fijamos en la historia social y arquitectónica de la región. Diseccionamos estos acontecimientos y los periodos que nos parecen más adecuados para el proyecto y para nosotros.

2. Hay varios factores que no pueden dejarse de lado. La historia del lugar, el programa, el cual está casi siempre estipulado por el cliente; y probablemente el factor más importante sea la escala de valores del cliente y cómo esta se corresponde con la nuestra.

3. Todas. Una casa no está formada por una serie de diseños individuales, sino por un puzzle que une sus diferentes partes, así que una habitación no puede ser más importante que otra.

4. El solar y el tipo de proyecto dictan los materiales que utilizamos. También hay que tener en cuenta el presupuesto, ya que es muy importante a la hora de tomar decisiones.

1. Wir sehen uns die soziale und architektonische Geschichte der Region genau an und versuchen, die Ereignisse in Erfahrung zu bringen, die einen Teil dieser Geschichte bilden. Wir analysieren diese Ereignisse und Zeiträume, die uns für unsere Planung und uns selbst am angemessensten erscheinen.

2. Es gibt mehrere Faktoren, die man unbedingt berücksichtigen muss. Die Geschichte des Ortes, die notwendigen Wohnfunktionen, die fast immer vom Kunden festgelegt werden. Der wahrscheinlich wichtigste Faktor ist die Werteskala des Kunden und wie diese mit der unseren übereinstimmt.

3. Alle. Ein Haus besteht nicht aus einer Reihe von individuellen Entwürfen, sondern aus einem Puzzle, das seine verschiedenen Teile zusammenfügt. Deshalb kann ein Raum nicht wichtiger als ein anderer sein.

4. Das Grundstück und die Art des Bauvorhabens geben uns die Materialien vor, die wir benutzen. Man muss auch das Budget berücksichtigen, da es die Entscheidungen wesentlich beeinflusst.

Insite Architecture Design is a multi-disciplinary firm that groups architects, designers, and consultants into teams that encompass architecture, the environment, and design. The diverse talents include specialties in urban planning, architecture, landscape architecture, design, communication, and graphic design that work together to develop new environments and creative processes within the context of a global media and technology. They are considered neither modern nor neo-modern. Their approach is based on an optimistic vision of architecture, technology, and global culture.

Insite Architecture Design es una firma multidisciplinar que agrupa arquitectos, diseñadores y consultores en un equipo que aborda las áreas de arquitectura, medio ambiente y diseño. Los diversos talentos que componen el grupo, especializados en urbanismo, arquitectura, paisajismo, diseño, comunicación y diseño gráfico, trabajan juntos para desarrollar nuevos entornos y procesos de creación dentro de un contexto de globalización de medios y tecnología. No se consideran modernos, ni neomodernos. Su creencia parte de una visión optimista de la arquitectura, la tecnología y la cultura global.

Insite Architecture Design ist ein multidisziplinäres Unternehmen, in dem Architekten, Innenarchitekten und Berater innerhalb eines Netzes tätig sind, das sich mit den Bereichen Architektur, Umwelt und Design befasst. Die verschiedenen Mitarbeiter der Gruppe sind Spezialisten in Städtebau, Architektur, Landschaftsplanung, Innenarchitektur, Kommunikation und Grafik und arbeiten zusammen, um neue Umgebungen und Gestaltungsprozesse innerhalb eines Kontextes der Globalisierung der Mittel und Technologie zu schaffen. Sie halten an einer optimistischen Vision der Architektur, Technologie und der globalen Kultur fest.

The architect treated this house as if it were the framework of a car, in which the concept of luxury is signified by the austerity of its interior rather than by the excessive use of objects. The main exercise in this project consisted of paring down rather than adding. The simplicity of the space is enhanced by its geometry, where right angles, large windows, and light colors predominate. The design plan was executed inside a building whose two levels are connected by an attractive metal and wood stairway. The richness and warmth of the interior mainly stems from the wood details and the finish. The upper level, containing the master bedroom, makes a connection between the interior and the exterior. The wood extends from the private area, passes through the large window, and continues along the terrace. In this very austere space, a low cement wall defines the bathroom area, linking it to the main area. The only piece of furniture in this space is the bed, which faces the exterior terrace.

House in Kuessnacht

Samuel Lerch

Kuessnacht, Switzerland, 2003
Photos © Bruno Helbling / zapaimages

El arquitecto entiende esta casa como la estructura de un coche, en donde el concepto de lujo es el vacío más que el exceso de elementos en el interior del espacio. En este proyecto el principal ejercicio ha sido el de eliminar, más que el de añadir. La sobriedad del espacio resalta gracias a una geometría en la que predominan los ángulos rectos, los amplios ventanales y los colores claros. El programa de la vivienda se desarrolla en un volumen de dos plantas

Für den Architekten ist dieses Haus ein Skelett, das sich unter den Autos befindet, und in dem Luxus eher als Leere anstelle überladener Räume verstanden wird. Bei dieser Planung hat man mehr weggenommen als hinzugefügt. Die Schlichtheit der Räume wird durch eine Geometrie unterstrichen, in der die geraden Winkel, große Fenster und helle Farben vorherrschen. Die einzelnen Räume erstrecken sich über zwei Stockwerke, die durch

unidas por una sugerente escalera de metal y madera. Este material es el principal detalle de acabado que otorga riqueza y calidez al interior. La parte superior, que alberga la habitación principal, vincula el interior con el exterior. La madera se extiende desde la zona privada hasta la terraza, atravesando el ventanal. En este espacio de gran sobriedad destaca el muro a media altura de cemento que define la zona de lavabos, vinculada al espacio principal. El único mobiliario de esta zona es la cama, ubicada frente a la terraza exterior.

eine schön gestaltete Treppe aus Metall und Holz verbunden sind. Dieses Material ist das wichtigste Gestaltungselement, das das Innere reich und warm wirken lässt. Im Obergeschoss befindet sich das Wohnzimmer, das eine Verbindung zwischen innen und außen herstellt. Das Element Holz erstreckt sich von den Privaträumen über das große Fenster bis zur Terrasse. In diesem sehr schlicht gehaltenen Raum hebt sich eine Zementmauer auf halber Höhe ab, die die Bereiche der Badezimmer definiert, die mit dem Hauptraum verbunden sind. Das einzige Möbelstück hier ist das Bett selbst, das sich gegenüber der Terrasse befindet.

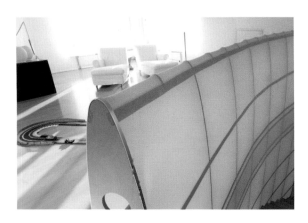

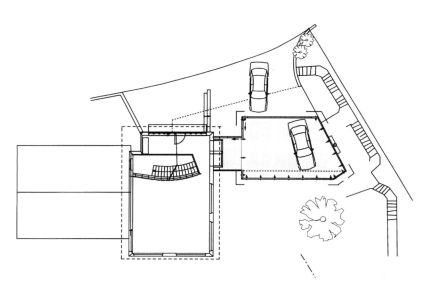

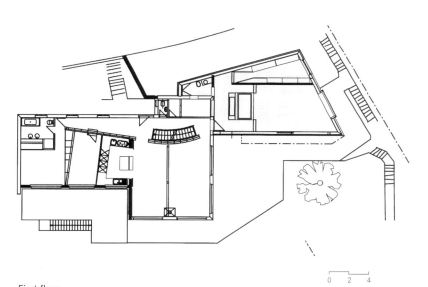

Ground floor

Planta baja

Erdgeschoss

First floor

Planta primera

Erster Stock

0 2 4

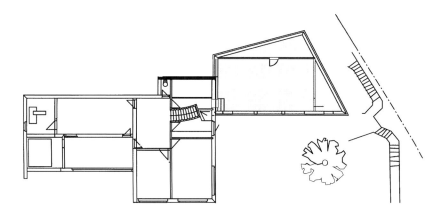

Second floor
Planta segunda
Zweiter Stock

1. What historical reference in particular inspires you when designing a residence?

¿Qué referente histórico en particular le sirve de fuente de inspiración a la hora de proyectar una vivienda?

Welche historische Referenz dient Ihnen als Inspiration beim Entwurf eines Hauses?

2. What is the main factor taken into consideration when designing a residence?

¿Cuál es el principal factor determinante a la hora de diseñar una vivienda?

Welche Rahmenbedingungen, bzw. Faktoren sind für Sie ausschlaggebend beim Konzipieren?

3. What room inside the home do you find most interesting to design?

¿Qué estancia de la vivienda encuentra usted más interesante para diseñar?

Welchen Raum des Hauses finden Sie am spannendsten zu entwerfen?

4. What is your criteria for choosing materials and finishings in a particular room?

¿Cuál es su criterio a la hora de seleccionar los materiales y los acabados en esta estancia?

Welche Kriterien wenden Sie bei der Entscheidung über Materialien und Oberflächen in diesem Raum an?

1. The straight-line style of the Bauhaus architects.

2. The design is determined by the future use of the space and by its surroundings.

3. The heart of the house, the place where people gather.

4. Light materials that are attractive and pleasing to the eye even after many years.

1. El estilo de líneas rectas de los arquitectos de la Bauhaus.

2. El espacio exterior existente y los futuros usos determinan el diseño.

3. El corazón de la casa, el centro de reunión social.

4. Materiales ligeros que resultan atractivos y agradables de ver incluso después de muchos años. La orientación natural de la luz, el juego cambiante de luces y sombras, que se continúa en la oscuridad con luz artificial.

1. Der geradlinige Stil der Bauhaus-Architekten.

2. Die Gestaltung wird von dem bereits existierenden Raum und der zukünftigen Nutzung bestimmt.

3. Das Herz des Hauses, der Ort, an dem sich die Menschen treffen.

4. Leichte Materialien, die sogar nach vielen Jahren noch angenehm und anziehend wirken.

Samuel Lerch was born in 1958, and received his architecture degree in 1980. During the first phase of his career he specialized in construction, working with several companies between 1981 and 1983. From 1984 to 1988 he was associated with various architectural and design offices, until he finally founded his own practice in Zurich in 1989. He mainly works on residential projects that involve new construction, but he also rehabilitates existing buildings, and does renovations and interior design.

Samuel Lerch nació en 1958 y se diplomó como arquitecto en 1980. En su primera fase de trabajo se centró en el campo de la construcción colaborando para varias empresas entre 1981 y 1983. Posteriormente, se dedicó a colaborar en varios despachos de arquitectura y diseño, entre 1984 y 1988, hasta fundar su propia oficina en Zurich, en 1989. Su trabajo se centra principalmente en proyectos de vivienda y comprende tanto proyectos de obra nueva como rehabilitaciones de edificios existentes, reformas y diseño de interiores.

Samuel Lerch wurde 1958 geboren und schloss 1980 sein Architekturstudium erfolgreich ab. In seiner ersten Arbeitsphase zwischen 1981 und 1983 arbeitete er für verschiedene Unternehmen im Bereich Konstruktion. Nachdem er dann zwischen 1984 und 1988 mit verschiedenen Architekturbüros zusammengearbeitet hatte, gründete er 1989 in Zürich sein eigenes Studio. Bei seiner Arbeit konzentriert er sich hauptsächlich auf Wohnhäuser, sowohl Neubauten als auch Umbauten bereits bestehender Gebäude, Renovierungen und Innenarchitektur.

A building that was abandoned for more than ten years served as the structural base for this project, which now contains three luxury apartments in the Islington neighborhood in Northwest London. An original aspect of this project is that all the units were individually designed to create a unique feeling in each through the use of light, color, and the layout of the space. Special attention was given to designing practical surroundings in the residence: large storage areas, intelligent lighting, sound systems, and bathrooms and kitchens equipped with the latest technical features. The lower apartments occupy a single level while the top one was designed to be spectacular with a double height ceiling. A large glass and steel canopy fills the entire ceiling and frames the view of the living room. The interior details and materials, dominated by stainless steel, wood, and glass, reinforce the impact of the space.

Shoreditch Conversion

Gregory Phillips Architects

London, UK, 2002
Photos © Paul Smoothy

Un edificio abandonado durante más de diez años sirvió como estructura base para crear este proyecto de vivienda que alberga ahora tres residencias de lujo en el barrio de Islington, en la parte nordeste de Londres. Un aspecto original de este proyecto es que cada una de las unidades fue diseñada individualmente para lograr producir en cada caso una atmósfera propia a través de la luz, el color y la disposición del espacio. Se prestó especial

Ein seit über zehn Jahren leer stehendes Gebäude war Gegenstand dieser Planung eines Wohnhauses, in dem drei Luxuswohnungen untergebracht sind. Es liegt im Nordosten Londons im Viertel Islington. Was dieses Gebäude sehr originell macht, ist die Tatsache, dass jede der Wohnungen individuell geplant wurde, um in jeder mithilfe des Lichtes, der Farben und der Anordnung der Räume eine eigene Atmosphäre zu schaffen. Besondere

atención en diseñar un entorno práctico para la vivienda: amplias zonas de almacenamiento, iluminación inteligente, equipos de sonido y baños y cocinas con la última tecnología incorporada. Las viviendas inferiores se plantean en una sola planta, mientras que la superior se diseñó como un volumen de doble altura de gran espectacularidad. Una gran marquesina de acero y cristal engloba la doble altura del espacio y enmarca la panorámica de la sala de estar de la vivienda. Los materiales y detalles interiores, en donde predomina el acero inoxidable, la madera y el cristal, acentúan la contundencia del espacio interior.

Aufmerksamkeit wurde beim Entwurf auf die praktische Umgebung der Wohnung gerichtet. So gibt es geräumige Aufbewahrungsbereiche, eine intelligente Beleuchtung, Tonsysteme, Bäder und Küchen, die mit den letzten technischen Neuheiten ausgestattet sind. Die Wohnungen der unteren Stockwerke liegen auf einer Etage, während die im letzten Stockwerk zweistöckig und besonders schön ist. Eine große Markise aus Stahl und Kristall umfasst die doppelte Höhe des Raumes und bildet einen Rahmen für das Wohnzimmer dieser Wohnung. Die Materialien und Elemente im Inneren, bei denen Edelstahl, Holz und Glas dominieren, unterstreichen noch die Wirkung der Räume.

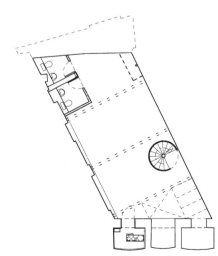
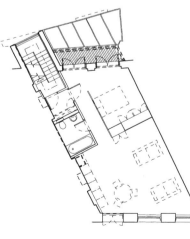
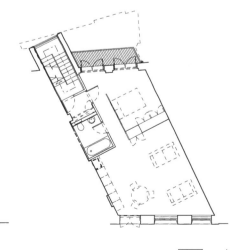

0 2 4

Basement plan

Planta sótano

Untergeschoss

Ground floor

Planta baja

Erdgeschoss

First floor

Planta primera

Erster Stock

Second floor

Planta segunda

Zweiter Stock

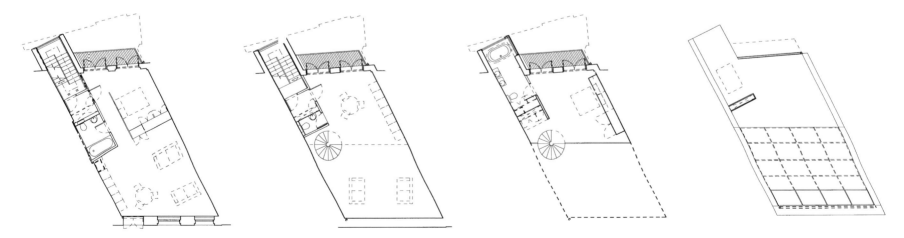

Third floor

Planta tercera

Dritter Stock

Fourth floor

Planta cuarta

Vierter Stock

Fifth floor

Planta quinta

Fünfter Stock

Roof plan

Planta de cubiertas

Dachgrundriss

0   2   4

1. What historical reference in particular inspires you when designing a residence?
¿Qué referente histórico en particular le sirve de fuente de inspiración a la hora de proyectar una vivienda?
Welche historische Referenz dient Ihnen als Inspiration beim Entwurf eines Hauses?

2. What is the main factor taken into consideration when designing a residence?
¿Cuál es el principal factor determinante a la hora de diseñar una vivienda?
Welche Rahmenbedingungen, bzw. Faktoren sind für Sie ausschlaggebend beim Konzipieren?

3. What room inside the home do you find most interesting to design?
¿Qué estancia de la vivienda encuentra usted más interesante para diseñar?
Welchen Raum des Hauses finden Sie am spannendsten zu entwerfen?

4. What is your criteria for choosing materials and finishings in a particular room?
¿Cuál es su criterio a la hora de seleccionar los materiales y los acabados en esta estancia?
Welche Kriterien wenden Sie bei der Entscheidung über Materialien und Oberflächen in diesem Raum an?

1. A house should be a sanctuary and a place that works for the owners; thus for me it is a combination of a temple, a machine for living in and the best most luxurious hotel.

2. It is a question of meeting the needs of the client, making the spaces work for their lifestyle and creating elegance. We also look to create wonderful spaces that make the most of the features of the site or building.

3. The living room and kitchen have to allow for many functions to occur. They are used throughout the day in various ways. These spaces are a fascinating challenge to create elegance, comfort and function.

4. Beauty, practicality, longevity.

1. Una casa debería ser una especie de santuario y un lugar práctico para los propietarios; por este motivo, constituye para mí la combinación de un templo, un aparato para vivir y el hotel más lujoso.

2. Es cuestión de conocer las necesidades del cliente, hacer que los espacios resulten útiles para su estilo de vida y crear elegancia. Asimismo, intentamos diseñar espacios maravillosos que aprovechen al máximo las características del solar o del edificio.

3. La sala de estar y la cocina deben albergar muchas funciones, ya que se utilizan durante el día de diversas maneras. Estos espacios son especialmente fascinantes a la hora de crear ambientes elegantes, confortables y funcionales.

4. Belleza, funcionalidad y durabilidad.

1. Ein Haus sollte eine Art heiliger Ort, aber auch ein praktischer Ort für die Besitzer sein. Deshalb ist es eine Kombination aus Tempel, Wohnapparat und Luxushotel.

2. Man muss die Bedürfnisse des Kunden kennen, und nützliche Räume für seinen Lebensstil und gleichzeitig Eleganz schaffen. Wir versuchen auch wundervolle Räume zu gestalten, mit denen wir die Möglichkeiten des Grundstückes oder des Hauses voll ausschöpfen. Vielleicht große Fenster, um den Ausblick zu genießen oder Räume doppelter Höhe, die die wichtigen Aspekte des Gebäudes miteinander verbinden.

3. Das Wohnzimmer und die Küche müssen vielen Funktionen dienen, da sie im Laufe des Tages auf verschiedene Weise genutzt werden. Diese Räume sind besonders interessant bei der Gestaltung eleganter, komfortabler und funktioneller Wohnatmosphären.

4. Schönheit, Funktionalität und Dauerhaftigkeit.

Gregory Phillips Architects is a young firm based in London. It consists of Gregory Phillips, who worked with David Chipperfield, and two other architects — Jay Salero, who practiced at Foster and Partners for three years, and Cathy Curran, a collaborator of Richard Rogers for four years — who act as project directors. Phillips, who founded his own office in 1991, is a devotee of esthetics and modern technology, and of developing any project of any scale.

Gregory Phillips Architects es una firma joven con sede en Londres. El propio Gregory Phillips es parte integrante, quien trabajó con David Chipperfield, y otros dos arquitectos como directores de proyectos: Jay Salero, que trabajó en Foster and Partners durante tres años, y Cathy Curran, que colaboró con Richard Rogers durante cuatro años. Phillips, quien fundó su propia oficina en 1991, es un devoto de la estética y la tecnología moderna y en la creación de cualquier proyecto a cualquier escala.

Gregory Phillips Architects ist ein junges Architekturbüro mit Sitz in London. Hier arbeiten Gregory Phillips selbst, der auch mit David Chipperfield kollaboriert hatte, und weitere Architekten, die verschiedene Projektleitungen übernehmen, nämlich Jay Salero, der drei Jahre lang bei Foster and Partners arbeitete, und Cathy Curran, die vier Jahre mit Richard Rogers zusammenarbeitete. Phillips, der sein Unternehmen 1991 gründete, liebt die Ästhetik und moderne Technologie und er sieht es als eine Herausforderung an, jegliches Projekt jeder Größenordnung zu übernehmen.

This residential project in Barcelona consisted of renovating the upper level of an old industrial building with a pitched roof. The original space had a large ground floor and a small top floor with access to a terrace. The primary objectives were to flood the space with natural light and to create spacious rooms. A large skylight was installed over the living and dining areas while other smaller openings were made to illuminate the bathrooms. The framework crossing the grand central skylight causes the light to reflect in several directions, creating a changing environment throughout the day. The layout of the space is organized around a furniture element that separates the night area from the day area. It does not reach as far as the ceiling or to the outside walls of the apartment, a feature that emphasizes the fluidity of the space. The piece serves as a shelf on the social side and as a closet on the private side. The communication between the sleeping area and the salon, or between the salon and the kitchen, is more flexible and striking because of the sliding doors.

Residence in Gracia

Sandra Aparicio + Forteza Carbonell Associats

Barcelona, Spain, 2002
Photos © Santiago Garcès

El proyecto de esta vivienda consistió en la reforma de un ático, con cubierta a dos aguas, en un antiguo edificio industrial de Barcelona. El espacio original contaba con una amplia superficie en la planta baja y una pequeña planta superior que daba acceso a una terraza. El principal objetivo era el de inundar el espacio con luz natural y crear estancias muy amplias. Para lograrlo se creó un gran lucernario que marcara la zona de estar y comedor,

Diese Wohnung entstand durch die Renovierung eines Penthouses mit Satteldach in einem alten Industriegebäude in Barcelona. Die Originalräume besaßen ein geräumiges Erdgeschoss und ein kleines Obergeschoss mit Zugang zur Terrasse. Vor allem wollte man viel Tageslicht in die Räume bringen und sie weitläufig wirken lassen. Dazu wurde ein großes Dachfenster eingebaut, das zu einem prägenden Element im

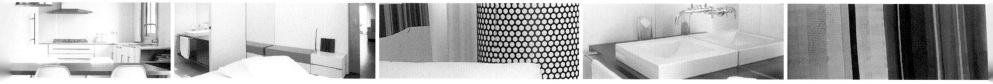

mientras que otras aberturas más pequeñas iluminaran los baños. Las intersecciones que atraviesan el gran lucernario central contribuyen a que la luz se refleje de diversas maneras y cree atmósferas variadas durante el día. El espacio se organiza a partir de un mueble central que separa la zona diurna de la nocturna y no llega a tocar el techo ni el perímetro de la vivienda, de esta manera ensalza la fluidez del espacio. El mueble funciona como estantería en la zona social y como armario para el ámbito privado. La relación entre la zona de dormir y el salón, o entre el salón y la cocina, se vuelve más flexible y contundente gracias a las puertas correderas.

Wohnzimmer und Esszimmer wurde. Die Helligkeit dringt durch kleinere Fenster in die Bäder ein. Die Schnittstellen, die sich durch das große zentrale Dachfenster ziehen, verursachen verschiedene Lichtreflexe, die die Stimmung in den Räumen im Laufe des Tages sehr verändern. Der Raum organisiert sich um ein zentrales Möbelstück herum, das die Bereiche für den Tag und die Nacht trennt und weder die Decke noch die Wände der Wohnung berührt, so dass der Raum sehr fließend wirkt. Zum Wohnbereich hin dient dieses Möbel als Regal, zu den Schlafzimmern hin als Schrank. Die Beziehung zwischen den Schlafzimmern und dem Wohnzimmern und zwischen dem Wohnzimmer und der Küche wird durch Schiebetüren noch flexibler und fließender.

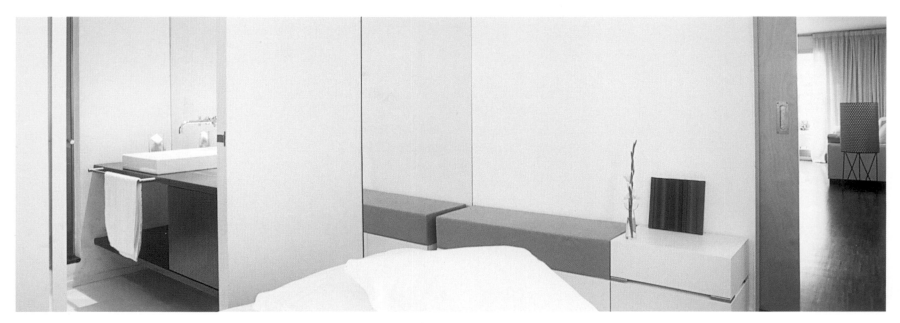

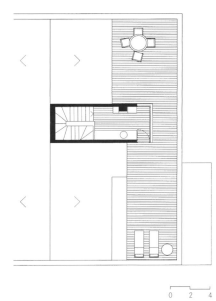

0   2   4

Plan

Planta

Grundriss

Roof plan

Planta de cubierta

Dachgrundriss

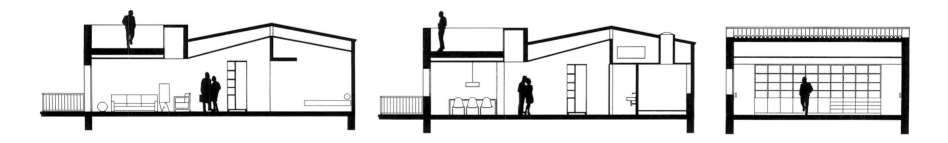

0 1 2

Sections

Secciones

Schnitte

1. What historical reference in particular inspires you when designing a residence?
¿Qué referente histórico en particular le sirve de fuente de inspiración a la hora de proyectar una vivienda?
Welche historische Referenz dient Ihnen als Inspiration beim Entwurf eines Hauses?

2. What is the main factor taken into consideration when designing a residence?
¿Cuál es el principal factor determinante a la hora de diseñar una vivienda?
Welche Rahmenbedingungen, bzw. Faktoren sind für Sie ausschlaggebend beim Konzipieren?

3. What room inside the home do you find most interesting to design?
¿Qué estancia de la vivienda encuentra usted más interesante para diseñar?
Welchen Raum des Hauses finden Sie am spannendsten zu entwerfen?

4. What is your criteria for choosing materials and finishings in a particular room?
¿Cuál es su criterio a la hora de seleccionar los materiales y los acabados en esta estancia?
Welche Kriterien wenden Sie bei der Entscheidung über Materialien und Oberflächen in diesem Raum an?

1. We find inspiration in different historical periods, probably because our projects are more related to interior design.

2. Fulfilling the functional requirements and the location of the project.

3. The living room is where people spend most of their time, so it is probably there that the overall feeling of the house can be summed up.

4. We usually choose three or four materials that are carried through all the rooms in the house. They always tend to be high quality materials.

1 Encontramos referencias en distintos momentos históricos, probablemente porque nuestros proyectos son más de interiorismo.

2. El programa funcional requerido y el lugar en el que esta se ubica.

3. El salón es el lugar en el que se acostumbra a estar más horas, en el que probablemente puedes sintetizar la atmósfera general de la vivienda.

4. Habitualmente decidimos tres o cuatro materiales y los repetimos en todas las estancias de la vivienda. Acostumbran a ser siempre materiales nobles.

1. Vielleicht finden wir deshalb zu verschiedenen Zeitpunkten der Geschichte Referenzen, weil unsere Projekte sich mehr mit der Innenarchitektur beschäftigen.

2. Das notwendige Wohnprogramm und der Standort.

3. Das Wohnzimmer ist der Ort, in dem man sich meistens mehr Stunden aufzuhalten pflegt, und in dem man die allgemeine Atmosphäre des Hauses oder der Wohnung zusammenfassen kann.

4. Normalerweise entscheiden wir uns für drei oder vier Materialien und wiederholen diese in allen Räumen der Wohnung. Wir arbeiten meist mit edlen Materialien.

Ignacio Forteza of Forteza Carbonell Associats, and Sandra Aparicio have collaborated on interior design projects since 1995. Forteza Carbonell Associats also does architectural design. Their work is based on respect and function, interpreting the needs of the client and trying to impart a magical sense to the spaces that will provoke thinking. The use of materials in their original form, and a careful execution of the construction is characteristic of their work.

Ignacio Forteza, del equipo Forteza Carbonell Associats, y Sandra Aparicio colaboran juntos desde 1995 en el campo del diseño interior. Asimismo, Forteza Carbonell Associats trabaja a su vez en el campo de la arquitectura. La labor que desarrollan parte del respeto y la funcionalidad del trabajo. Interpretan las necesidades del cliente e intentan aportar una mirada mágica a los espacios y volverlos sugerentes. Los rasgos característicos de sus obras son la utilización de materiales en estado primitivo y la cuidada ejecución en la edificación.

Ignacio Forteza von Forteza Carbonell Associats und Sandra Aparicio arbeiten schon seit 1995 bei der Gestaltung von Innenräumen zusammen. Forteza Carbonell Associats beschäftigt sich auch mit Architektur. Die Arbeitsphilosophie dieser Architekten stützt sich auf die Pfeiler Respekt und Funktionalität. Sie interpretieren die Bedürfnisse ihrer Kunden und versuchen die Räume magisch und suggestiv zu gestalten. Typisch für ihre Planungen ist die Verwendung von Materialien in ihrem ursprünglichen Zustand und eine sehr sorgfältiges Arbeiten beim Bau.

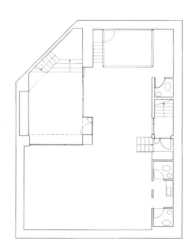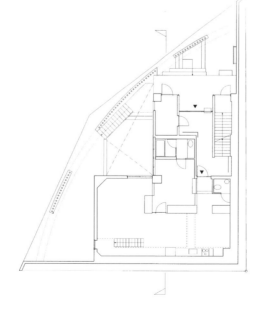

Basement

Planta sótano

Untergeschoss

Ground floor

Planta baja

Erdgeschoss

First floor

Planta primera

Erster Stock

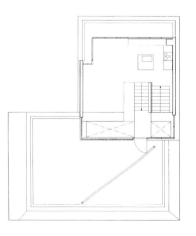

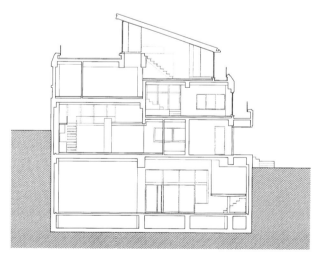

Second floor

Planta segunda

Zweiter Stock

Section

Sección

Schnitt

0 2 4

1. What historical reference in particular inspires you when designing a residence?
¿Qué referente histórico en particular le sirve de fuente de inspiración a la hora de proyectar una vivienda?
Welche historische Referenz dient Ihnen als Inspiration beim Entwurf eines Hauses?

2. What is the main factor taken into consideration when designing a residence?
¿Cuál es el principal factor determinante a la hora de diseñar una vivienda?
Welche Rahmenbedingungen, bzw. Faktoren sind für Sie ausschlaggebend beim Konzipieren?

3. What room inside the home do you find most interesting to design?
¿Qué estancia de la vivienda encuentra usted más interesante para diseñar?
Welchen Raum des Hauses finden Sie am spannendsten zu entwerfen?

4. What is your criteria for choosing materials and finishings in a particular room?
¿Cuál es su criterio a la hora de seleccionar los materiales y los acabados en esta estancia?
Welche Kriterien wenden Sie bei der Entscheidung über Materialien und Oberflächen in diesem Raum an?

1. Ways that the nature has been incorporated in architectures in the past is the historical reference that inspires us the most such as use of natural light and wind.

2. The majority of our work has been residences in urban area. Thus, the main factor that is taken consideration when designing a residence is how we can incorporate a life style of a resident to town space.

3. Our interest expands beyond designing a particular room. We are rather interested in continuity of rooms and spaces of a house.

4. We do not choose materials not only by their looks and colors but also by their touch, feel, acoustic quality, and combination of materials.

1. La referencia histórica que más nos inspira es la forma en la que la naturaleza se ha incorporado a la arquitectura en el pasado, por ejemplo, con la incorporación del viento y la luz natural.

2. La mayoría de nuestros trabajos han sido residencias urbanas. Por esta razón, nuestra mayor preocupación cuando diseñamos un espacio consiste en intentar incorporar el estilo de vida de sus habitantes en el espacio urbano.

3. Nuestros intereses se extienden más allá del diseño de una habitación en particular. Estamos más interesados en la continuidad entre las habitaciones y los espacios de la vivienda.

4. No elegimos los materiales solamente por su aspecto y color, sino por su tacto, calidad acústica y la combinación con los otros materiales.

1. Die historische Referenz, die uns am meisten inspiriert, ist die Art und Weise, wie man die Natur in die Architektur der Vergangenheit integriert hat, zum Beispiel, wie mit dem Wind oder dem Tageslicht umgegangen wurde.

2. Die meisten unserer Arbeiten sind städtische Wohnhäuser. Deshalb ist es für uns bei der Gestaltung eines Raumes sehr wichtig, den Lebensstil seiner Bewohner in die städtische Umgebung zu integrieren.

3. Unsere Interessen gehen weit über die Gestaltung eines speziellen Raumes hinaus. Uns interessiert die Kontinuität zwischen den Zimmern und Räumen einer Wohnung.

4. Wir wählen die Materialien nicht allein aufgrund ihres Aussehens und ihrer Farbe aus, sondern auch danach, wie sie sich anfühlen, nach ihren akustischen Eigenschaften und wie sie sich mit anderen Materialien kombinieren lassen.

Yasushi Ikeda was born in 1961 in Fukuoka. He studied in the Architecture School at the University of Tokyo and worked in the architectural office of Maki and Associates (1987-1995). Later, he established Ikeda Design Studio. Since 1996 he is an assistant professor in the School of Environmental Information in Keio University.
Akiko Kokubun was born in 1965 in Tokyo. She studied in the Architecture School at the University of Tokyo and worked in the architectural office of Maki and Associates (1988-1997). In 1997 she joined the Ikeda Kokubun Design Studio.

Yasushi Ikeda nació en Fukuoka en 1961. Estudió en el departamento de arquitectura de la Universidad de Tokio y trabajó en la oficina de arquitectura Maki and Associates (1987-1995). Posteriomente, estableció Ikeda Design Studio. Desde 1996 es profesor asistente en la Escuela de Información Mediambiental, en la Universidad de Keio.
Akiko Kokubun nació en Tokio en 1965. Estudió en la facultad de arquitectura de la Universidad de Tokio y trabajó en la oficina de arquitectura Maki and Associates (1988-1997). En 1997 se asoció a Ikeda Kokubun Design Studio.

Yasushi Ikeda kam 1961 in Fukuoka zur Welt. Er studierte Architektur an der Universität von Tokio und arbeitete in dem Unternehmen Maki and Associates (1987-1995). Später gründete er Ikeda Design Studio. Seit 1996 ist er assistierender Professor an der Fakultät für Umweltinformation der Keio Universität.
Akiko Kokubun kam 1965 in Tokio zur Welt. Sie studierte Architektur an der Universität von Tokio und arbeitete in dem Unternehmen Maki and Associates (1988-1997). 1997 wurde sie Mitbegründerin des Kokubun Design Studios.

The history of this project began with the need to cover the top floor of this building in order to protect the lower levels from the elements. The resulting space was later occupied by separate, individual structures. In their approach to the renovation project the architects used this concept as a point of departure to create a residence based on minimal units that were developed according to a mutual relationship. The placement of the units was based on geometric shapes that break up the building's existing straight lines. This manipulation of form helps direct the eye towards distant views, beyond the surrounding neighbors. The interior units can be expanded and adapted according to specific needs using textile panels that slide on rails. These elements can also be folded so that the spaces can almost entirely be integrated. The roof extends beyond the sides of the building to create overhanging glass projections, which show the interior work while covering projections from the lower floors of the building.

Rooftop

Holodeck.at

Vienna, Austria, 2002
Photos © Veronika Hofinger

La historia de este proyecto comienza con la necesidad de cubrir la última planta de este edificio con el fin de proteger las plantas inferiores de las condiciones climáticas. El espacio resultante fue posteriormente ocupado por elementos concretos e individuales. Al abordar el proyecto de reforma, los arquitectos tomaron este concepto como punto de partida para la creación de una vivienda basada en unidades mínimas que se desarrollan entre sí.

Die Grundlage dieser Planung war die Notwendigkeit, das Dach eines letzten Stockwerkes zu decken, um die unteren Stockwerke vor Wettereinflüssen zu schützen. Der dadurch entstandene Raum wurde allmählich von einzelnen, individuellen Elementen eingenommen. Die Architekten betrachteten dieses Renovierungsprojekt als Ausgangspunkt für die Erschaffung eines Wohnraumes, der auf minimalen Einheiten basiert, die sich gemeinsam

La disposición de las unidades parte de una geometría que rompe con las líneas ortogonales del edificio existente. Con este gesto formal se logra conducir la mirada hacia panorámicas muy lejanas, por encima del vecindario circundante. Las unidades interiores se pueden ampliar y adaptar según el uso específico gracias a paneles textiles que se deslizan sobre rieles. Estos elementos pueden también ser plegados y lograr así que la integración de las unidades sea prácticamente total. La cubierta se extiende por fuera de los límites de la vivienda en forma de voladizos de cristal, que evidencian la intervención interior y cubren las proyecciones del volumen del edificio en plantas inferiores.

entwickeln. Die Anordnung der Teile geht von einer Geometrie aus, die die rechtwinkligen Linien des existierenden Gebäudes bricht. Mit dieser formalen Geste wird der Blick auf das weit entfernte Panorama gelenkt, über den umgebenden Gebäuden gelegen. Die inneren Einheiten können mithilfe von Stoffpaneelen, die auf Führungen verschoben werden, für die jeweilige Nutzung erweitert oder verändert werden. Diese Elemente können auch gefaltet werden, so dass die Einheiten praktisch zu einem einzigen Raum werden können. Das Dach erstreckt sich außerhalb der Wohnung in Form von gläsernen Vorsprüngen, und zeigt somit die äußeren und inneren Eingriffe und deckt gleichzeitig die Wohnung und die unteren Stockwerke des Gebäudes.

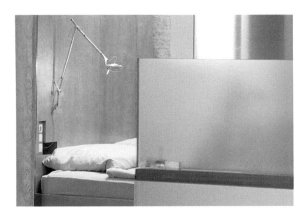

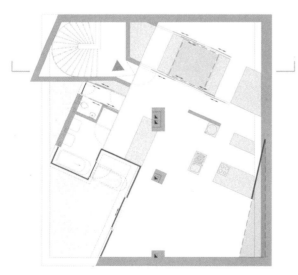
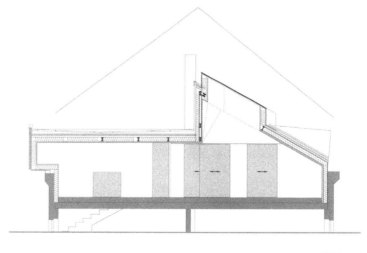

0 1 2

Ground floor

Planta baja

Erdgeschoss

Section

Sección

Schnitt

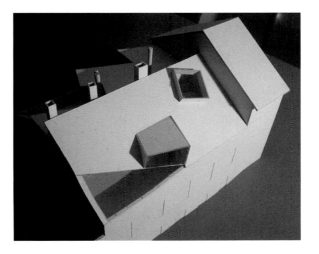

Model
Modelo
Modell

1. What historical reference in particular inspires you when designing a residence?
¿Qué referente histórico en particular le sirve de fuente de inspiración a la hora de proyectar una vivienda?
Welche historische Referenz dient Ihnen als Inspiration beim Entwurf eines Hauses?

2. What is the main factor taken into consideration when designing a residence?
¿Cuál es el principal factor determinante a la hora de diseñar una vivienda?
Welche Rahmenbedingungen, bzw. Faktoren sind für Sie ausschlaggebend beim Konzipieren?

3. What room inside the home do you find most interesting to design?
¿Qué estancia de la vivienda encuentra usted más interesante para diseñar?
Welchen Raum des Hauses finden Sie am spannendsten zu entwerfen?

4. What is your criteria for choosing materials and finishings in a particular room?
¿Cuál es su criterio a la hora de seleccionar los materiales y los acabados en esta estancia?
Welche Kriterien wenden Sie bei der Entscheidung über Materialien und Oberflächen in diesem Raum an?

---

1. The continuity and complexity of spaces and the social interactivity in the historical 'medina' as well as the principle of the courtyard house.

2. The adaption of the program 'housing' to the complexity of the clients desires combined with the particularities of the site.

3. The continuum of spaces and their flexible arrangement following the functional and emotional demands of the client.

4. To emphasize the conceptual idea.

---

1. La continuidad y complejidad de los espacios y la interactividad social en la histórica medina como concepto de casa ajardinada.

2. La adaptación del programa a la complejidad de los deseos de los clientes combinada con las particularidades del solar.

3. La continuidad de espacios y su distribución flexible siguiendo las demandas funcionales y emocionales del cliente.

4. Acentuar la idea abstracta.

---

1. Die Kontinuität und die Vielschichtigkeit der Räume und die soziale Dialogfähigkeit in den historischen, arabischen Altstädten als das Konzept eines Hauses mit Garten.

2. Die Anpassung der Wohnprogramme an die Vielschichtigkeit der Wünsche der Kunden in Kombination mit den Eigenschaften des Grundstückes.

3. Die Kontinuität der Räume und die flexible Verteilung, die den funktionellen und emotionalen Wünschen des Kunden entspricht.

4. Die abstrakte Idee unterstreichen.

Holodeck.at is a design office founded in 1998 by Marlies Breuss, Michael Ogertsching and Susanne Schmall. She left the firm at the beginning of 2001, gaining additional experience at studios in Los Angeles, Barcelona, and Tokyo. Her philosophy is based on a conceptual and logical plan that focuses on restructuring projects and developing specific functions. Holodeck.at creates the design tools required for their projects by collecting and researching information on the particular location.

Holodeck.at es una oficina de diseño fundada en 1998 por Marlies Breuss, Michael Ogertsching y Susanne Schmall. A principios de 2001 Susanne Schmall deja la firma, y su experiencia se enriquece con estudios en Los Ángeles, Barcelona y Tokio. Su filosofía parte de un esquema conceptual y programático en donde se ocupa principalmente de la reestructuración de programas y el desarrollo de funciones específicas. Holodeck.at obtiene las herramientas de diseño para sus encargos gracias al almacenamiento y a la filtración de informaciones de un lugar concreto.

Holodeck.at ist ein Architekturbüro, das von Marlies Breuss, Michael Ogertsching und Susanne Schmall 1998 gegründet wurde. Susanne Schmall verließ die Firma 2001. Die Architekten haben durch Studien in Los Angeles, Barcelona und Tokio Erfahrung gesammelt. Die Unternehmensphilosophie beruht auf einem konzeptuellen und programmatischen Schema, hauptsächlich widmet man sich der Neustrukturierung von Wohnräumen und der Entwicklung spezifischer Funktionen. Durch das Speichern und Filtern von Informationen über den Standort werden die Gestaltungswerkzeuge für die einzelnen Aufträge geschaffen.

La ubicación del Ray 1, en la última planta de un edificio de oficinas de la década de 1960, y en el corazón del cuarto distrito de Viena, sirve como referente y estímulo para el desarrollo del proyecto. El diseño, que inevitablemente debía conciliar las estrictas regulaciones con respecto a las cubiertas de edificios, no cae en los tópicos encasillamientos, sino que se plantea como una reinterpretación de este tipo de regulaciones. Para poder

eines Bürogebäudes aus den Sechzigerjahren, inmitten des vierten Bezirks von Wien, diente als Referenzpunkt und Inspiration für Durchführung des Projektes. Bei der Gestaltung konnten die strengen Verordnungen für die Gestaltung der Dächer nicht umgangen werden. Diese werden jedoch nicht als Einschränkungen aufgefasst, sondern sie werden einfach auf kreative Weise neu interpre-

trasladar el concepto de diseño a la estructura original del edificio, se optó por un esqueleto de acero que permite distribuir las cargas de una manera homogénea a los muros del edificio. Las cargas principales las recibe el hastial, mientras que los demás elementos metálicos sirven como marcos para un envoltorio de cristal. El resultado es de una ligereza sorprendente y crea un objeto de particular interés en relación con el entorno urbano más inmediato. La propia forma de la estructura así como la permanente relación con el paisaje circundante crean una atmósfera dinámica en su interior y una oportunidad para experimentar el exterior a modo de terrazas o grandes aberturas.

tiert. Um das Designkonzept auf die Originalstruktur des Gebäudes übertragen zu können, wurde ein Stahlskelett gewählt, über das die Lasten gleichmäßig auf die Mauern des Gebäudes übertragen werden. Die Hauptlasten werden von der Seitenwand getragen, während die übrigen Elemente aus Metall als Rahmen für die Hülle aus Glas dienen. Das Ergebnis wirkt überraschend leicht und es entstand ein Objekt, das in seiner unmittelbaren Umgebung sehr interessant wirkt. Die Form der Struktur selbst und die ständige Beziehung zu der umgebenden Landschaft schaffen eine dynamische Atmosphäre im Inneren und geben die Möglichkeit, außen mithilfe von Terrassen und großen Öffnungen zu experimentieren.

The location of the Ray 1 project, on the top floor of a 1960's office building in the center of Vienna's fourth district, served as a reference and an inspiration for the design of the project. The architect's design, which inevitably had to take into account the strict regulations regarding the coverings of buildings, did not fit into the typical mold, but was approached as a reinterpretation of these kinds of regulations. In order to apply the design concept, a steel skeleton was used to evenly distribute the load on the building's original structure. The gable carries the main weight while the other metal parts act as frames for the glass covering. The result is surprisingly light and creates a structure that is particularly interesting in relation to the surrounding urban setting. The form of the structure itself, as well as the permanent relationship with the surrounding landscape, creates a dynamic atmosphere in the interior and an opportunity to experience the outside from terraces or through large openings.

Ray 1

Delugan_Meissl

Vienna, Austria, 2003
Photos © Rupert Steiner

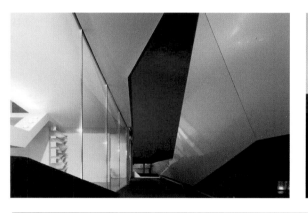

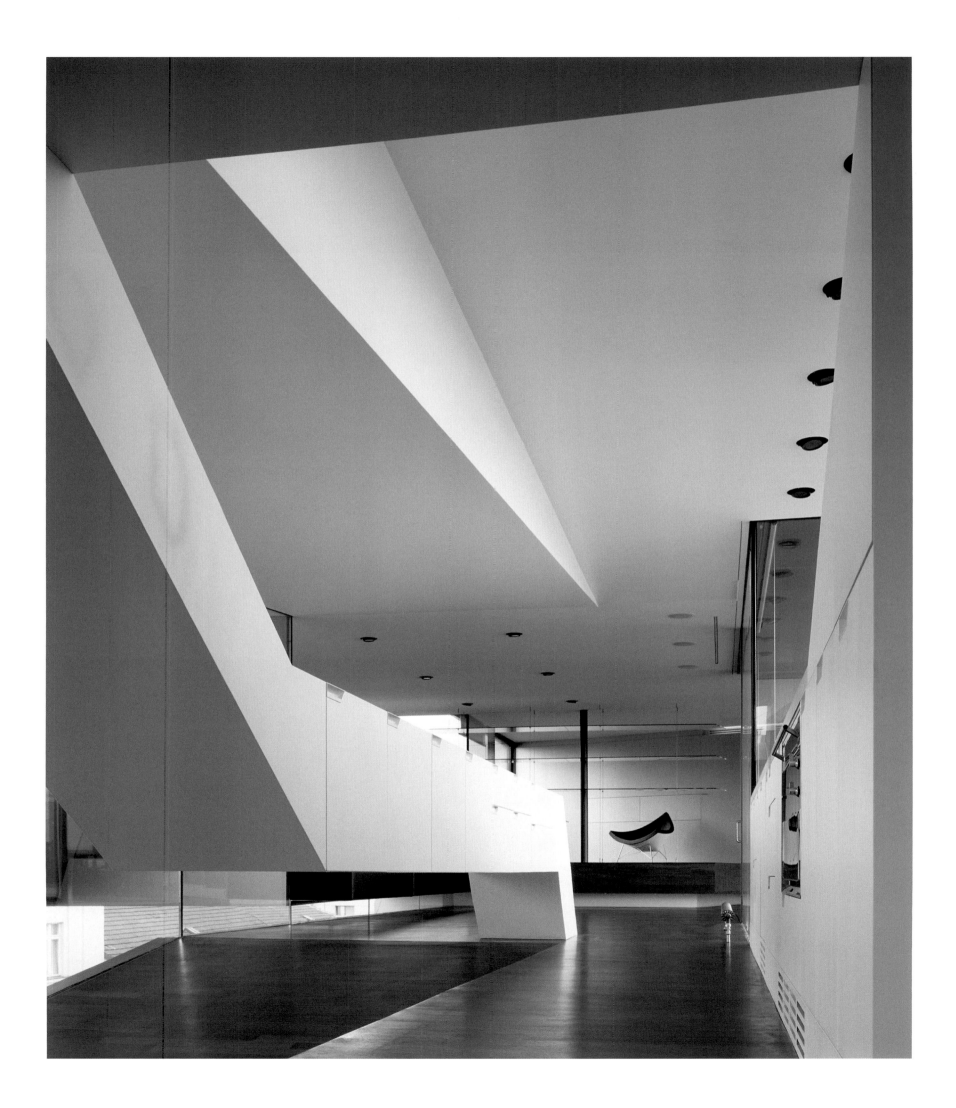

1. What historical reference in particular inspires you when designing a residence?

   ¿Qué referencia histórico en particular le sirve de fuente de inspiración a la hora de proyectar una vivienda?

   Welche historische Referenz dient Ihnen als Inspiration beim Entwurf eines Hauses?

2. What is the main factor taken into consideration when designing a residence?

   ¿Cuál es el principal factor determinante a la hora de diseñar una vivienda?

   Welche Rahmenbedingungen, bzw. Faktoren sind für Sie ausschlaggebend beim Konzipieren?

3. What room inside the home do you find most interesting to design?

   ¿Qué estancia de la vivienda encuentra usted más interesante para diseñar?

   Welchen Raum des Hauses finden Sie am spannendsten zu entwerfen?

4. What is your criteria for choosing materials and finishings in a particular room?

   ¿Cuál es su criterio a la hora de seleccionar los materiales y los acabados en esta estancia?

   Welche Kriterien wenden Sie bei der Entscheidung über Materialien und Oberflächen in diesem Raum an?

---

1. The architecture of Oscar Niemeyer and John Lautner.

2. In our concepts a building is always conceived as one aspect of something greater as existing within a spatial context. The design has its starting point in the genius loci.

3. A combination of living room and kitchen — we find it highly interesting how rooms interact with each other and how we could achieve the interior space as a flowing internal continuum whose various functional areas are defined by different floor levels, zones, or niches without using spatial or visual separators.

4. The materials we choose reflect and support the specific demanded use of each particular room and their haptic dimension is very important to us. In most cases we use materials in their original colour in order to give a starting point for an individual colourful occupation.

---

1. La arquitectura de Oscar Niemeyer y John Lautner.

2. En nuestros conceptos, un edificio siempre se concibe tanto como un elemento dentro de algo más grande que como pieza existente en un contexto espacial. El diseño tiene su punto de partida en el espíritu del lugar.

3. La combinación de sala de estar y cocina. Encontramos muy interesante el modo en que las diferentes habitaciones interactúan entre sí y cómo podemos conseguir que el espacio interior sea continuo, fluido y cuyas distintas áreas estén definidas por pavimentos, zonas o aberturas a diferentes niveles, sin necesidad de utilizar divisiones espaciales o visuales.

4 Los materiales que elegimos reflejan y acentúan el uso específico de cada habitación y su dimensión táctil es muy importante para nosotros. En la mayoría de los casos utilizamos los materiales con su color original con el fin de crear un punto de partida para una ocupación individual.

---

1. Die Architektur von Oscar Niemeyer und John Lautner.

2. Es ist unsere Auffassung, dass ein Gebäude immer als ein Element innerhalb einer existierenden, größeren Einheit in einem räumlichen Kontextes entworfen wird. Der Ausgangspunkt für die Gestaltung ist der Geist, der an dem Ort herrscht.

3. Eine Kombination von Wohnzimmer und Küche finden wir sehr interessant, da hier die verschiedenen Räume miteinander in Beziehung stehen. So wird ein durchgehender, fließender innerer Raum geschaffen, dessen verschiedenen Bereiche durch die Fußböden und Zonen oder Öffnungen auf verschiedener Höhe definiert sind, ohne dass dazu räumliche oder visuelle teilende Elemente notwendig sind.

4. Die von uns ausgewählten Materialien spiegeln die spezifische Nutzung jedes Zimmer wieder und verstärken sie. Die taktile Dimension ist uns sehr wichtig. In den meisten Fällen verwenden wir Materialien, ohne ihre Farbe zu verändern, um so einen Ausgangspunkt für eine individuelle Besetzung zu schaffen.

Elke Delugan-Meissl (Linz, Austria) and Roman Delugan (Merano, Italy) joined to found their own architectural office in 1993. If there is a principle that guides their design method it would probably be the landscape. For them, a building is always seen as another aspect of something much larger that forms part of a spatial context, and not just a single structure. The design of each element is approached as a synthesis of the setting, while attempting to contribute something that would complement it. Their work encompasses a wide range of residential projects.

Elke Delugan-Meissl (Linz, Austria) y Roman Delugan (Merano, Italia) se asociaron y fundaron su propio despacho de arquitectura en 1993. Si existiese un principio que guiara su método de diseño, sería probablemente el concepto de paisaje. Para ellos un edificio siempre está concebido como un aspecto más de algo mucho más grande que forma parte de un contexto espacial y no como una estructura solitaria. El diseño de cada elemento se plantea como una síntesis del entorno al tiempo que pretende contribuir a complementarlo. Su obra comprende una variada gama de proyectos residenciales.

Elke Delugan-Meissl (Linz, Österreich) und Roman Delugan (Meran, Italien) gründeten 1993 gemeinsam ein Architekturstudio. Falls es ein Prinzip gäbe, nach dem sich ihre Designmethode richtet, so wäre dies wahrscheinlich die Landschaft. Für diese Architekten ist ein Gebäude immer ein Aspekt einer größeren Einheit. Es gehört in einen räumlichen Kontext und ist keine einsame Struktur. Die Gestaltung jedes Elementes wird als die Synthese der Umgebung aufgefasst; gleichzeitig soll die Umgebung ergänzt werden. Sie haben bereits zahlreiche Projekte für Wohnanlagen verwirklicht.

Mark Mack, along with his former partner Andrew Batey, earned his reputation as an architect in California mainly for his single-family home and villa designs in the early 1980's. He established his own office in San Francisco in 1984 and then moved to Venice, California in 1993. His approach to design is influenced by his academic work and restless curiosity. He was a professor in the School of Architecture at the University of California, Los Angeles. He was also a cofounder of Archetype Magazine and has contributed numerous articles to different magazines.

Mark Mack, junto a su antiguo socio Andrew Batey, se ha ganado su reputación como arquitecto en California principalmente por el diseño de villas y casas unifamiliares al in cio de la década de 1980. Estableció su propia oficina en San Francisco en 1984 y posteriormente se desplazó a Venice, California, en 1993. Su acercamiento al diseño está influenciado por sus inquietudes y su trabajo académico. Fue prcfesor de la Escuela de Arquitectura en la Universidad de California, Los Ángeles; asimismo fue cofundador de la revista Archetype Magazine y colaborador en numerosos artículos en diversas publicaciones.

Mark Mack begann seine Karriere Anfang der Achtzigerjahre mit der Planung von Einfamilienhäusern und Villen in Kalifornien zusammen mit seinem ehemaligen Teilhaber Andrew Batey. 1984 gründete er in San Francisco sein eigenes Unternehmen, das er 1993 nach Venice, Kalifornien, verlegte. Seine Interessen und seine akademische Arbeit beeinflussen stark seinen Gestaltungsstil. Er war Professor am Fachbereich Architektur der Universität von Kalifornien in Los Angeles. Ebenso ist er Mitbegründer der Zeitschrift Archetype Magazine, in der er zahlreiche Artikel veröffentlicht hat.

APARTMENTS

APARTAMENTOS / WOHNUNGEN

Olympic Tower Residence

House T

London Mews Conversion

Flatiron District Loft

Flexible Loft

Sempacher Apartments

Loft in Tribeca

Small Loft in Vienna

Lords Telephone Exchange

House in the Coast

Plan

Planta

Grundriss

After finishing his studies at the Rhode Island School of Design in 1980 and complementing them at the Architectural Association of London, Michael Gabellini founded Gabellini Associates en 1991. Gabellini is known for his luxurious, elegant designs in which space and light are the main components. He has designed several boutiques for the most prestigious companies of the fashion world. His studies in art led him to carry out several projects for galleries and museums. In residential design he uses an esthetic that mixes the sophisticated and the casual to create a comfortable environment.

Después de estudiar arquitectura en la Escuela de Diseño de Rhode Island en 1980 y ce haberlos complementado en la Architectural Association de Londres, Michael Gabellini fundó la firma Gabellini Associates en 1991. Gabellini es conocido por su diseño lujoso y elegante, donde la luz y el espacio son los principales materiales. En el campo de la moda ha diseñando varias boutiques para las más prestigiosas firmas. Su investigación en el arte lo ha llevado a realizar varios proyectos para museos y galerías. En el diseño de residencias utiliza una estética que mezcla sofisticación y casualidad para crear un entorno confortable.

Nach dem Michael Gabellini 1980 sein Architekturstudium an der Rhode Island School of Design abgeschlossen hatte, und sich an der Architectural Association in London weitergebildet hatte, gründete er 1991 Gabellini Associates. Gabellini ist für luxuriöse, elegante und elementaren Entwürfe bekannt, in denen Licht und Raum die wichtigsten Elemente sind. Aufgrund seines Interesses für die moderne Kunst hat er auch verschiedene Projekte für Museen und Galerien durchgeführt. Die von ihm gestalteten Wohnungen zeichnen dadurch aus, dass sie Edles mit spontaneren Elementen verbinden.

1. What historical reference in particular inspires you when designing a residence?
¿Qué referente histórico en particular le sirve de fuente de inspiración a la hora de proyectar una vivienda?
Welche historische Referenz dient Ihnen als Inspiration beim Entwurf eines Hauses?

2. What is the main factor taken into consideration when designing a residence?
¿Cuál es el principal factor determinante a la hora de diseñar una vivienda?
Welche Rahmenbedingungen, bzw. Faktoren sind für Sie ausschlaggebend beim Konzipieren?

3. What room inside the home do you find most interesting to design?
¿Qué estancia de la vivienda encuentra usted más interesante para diseñar?
Welchen Raum des Hauses finden Sie am spannendsten zu entwerfen?

4. What is your criteria for choosing materials and finishings in a particular room?
¿Cuál es su criterio a la hora de seleccionar los materiales y los acabados en esta estancia?
Welche Kriterien wenden Sie bei der Entscheidung über Materialien und Oberflächen in diesem Raum an?

---

1. Perhaps it is the buildings that were constructed over generations without a particular plan. Houses that have been subject to changes, adaptations, and additions in response to the needs of their occupants. I find the pursuit of modernization, where form rigorously follows function, to be an overly confining, almost boring approach.

2. The location. The building can make the place and the place can make the building; I am interested in this type of dialogue.

3. Every connecting space in a house. The rooms that can survive without having a specific function designated by the contractor.

4. The most interesting secondary rooms are those that do not have to conform to any particular function or material. The unique characteristics of each room, together with a certain atmosphere, develop during the creative process.

---

1. Son quizás aquellas construcciones que desde varias generaciones se han levantando sin un plan general. Casas que han sufrido modificaciones, adaptaciones y ampliaciones en relación tanto con sus inquilinos como con su uso. La consecución de la modernidad, donde la forma ha de seguir rigurosamente la función, me parece demasiado encorsetado, casi aburrido.

2. El lugar. A mí me interesa esa dialéctica que un edificio puede hacer al lugar, así como el lugar hace al edificio.

3. Todos los espacios conectores de una casa. Son aquellas habitaciones de la vivienda que consiguen sobrevivir sin una función concreta frente al programa de ordenación del espacio del constructor.

4. Las estancias secundarias más interesantes son aquellas en las que no se ha de desarrollar un concepto de material único. A lo largo del proceso de creación van surgiendo las características específicas de cada habitación junto con una atmósfera determinada.

---

1. Vielleicht sind es diejenigen Bauwerke, welche ohne ersichtlichen Gesamtplan über mehrere Generationen entstanden sind. Häuser, welche sowohl bezüglich Nutzer wie auch bezüglich Nutzung Änderungen, Anpassungen und Erweiterungen erfahren haben. Die Forderung der Moderne, wo Form strikte der Funktion zu folgen hat, scheint mir zu eingengend, gar langweilig. Alles bleibt ablesbar und voraussehbar.

2. Der ORT. Mich interessiert diese Dialektik, dass ein Gebäude den Ort machen kann sowie eben auch der Ort das Gebäude macht.

3. Alle Zwischenräume eines Hauses. Es sind dies diejenigen Räume des Hauses, welche es gegenüber dem Raumprogramm des Bauherrn schaffen, ohne bestimmte Nutzungszuordnung zu überleben.

4. Die spannendsten Raumfolgen sind diejenigen, bei welchen nicht ein einheitliches Materialkonzept durchgezogen werden muss. Im Verlauf des Entwurfsprozesses schälen sich für die jeweiligen Räume spezifische Eigenschaften und schliesslich eine Atmosphäre heraus.

Leo Frei, founder of Frei Architekten, was born in Zurich in 1958, where he also pursued his architecture studies. After earning his degree in 1983 he added a Master of Architecture degree from the Technological Institute in Atlanta. After working in different architectural firms for several years he started his own office in 1991, in Zurich and Stäfa. He complements his work as an architect with academic duties as a professor, assistant, and instructor in various Swiss universities.

Leo Frei, fundador de Frei Architekten, nació en 1958 en Zurich, ciudad en donde adquirió sus estudios de arquitectura. Después de obtener su título en 1983, complementó sus estudios con un máster en Arquitectura en el Instituto Tecnológico de Atlanta. Tras colaborar durante varios años en diferentes despachos de arquitectura, fundó su propia oficina en 1991, en Zurich y Stäfa. Su trabajo como arquitecto lo complementa con su actividad docente como profesor, asistente y tutor en varias universidades suizas.

Leo Frei, der Gründer von Frei Architekten, kam 1958 in Zürich auf die Welt, wo er auch Architektur studierte. Nach Abschluss seines Diploms im Jahr 1983 erwarb er noch einen Master am Technological Institute in Atlanta. Nachdem er mehrere Jahre lang in verschiedenen Architekturbüros mitgearbeitet hatte, gründete er 1991 sein eigenes Unternehmen in Zürich und Stäfa. Seine Arbeit als Architekt ergänzt er mit seiner Lehrtätigkeit als Professor, Assistent und Tutor an verschiedenen Universitäten in der Schweiz.

1. What historical reference in particular inspires you when designing a residence?
¿Qué referente histórico en particular le sirve de fuente de inspiración a la hora de proyectar una vivienda?
Welche historische Referenz dient Ihnen als Inspiration beim Entwurf eines Hauses?

2. What is the main factor taken into consideration when designing a residence?
¿Cuál es el principal factor determinante a la hora de diseñar una vivienda?
Welche Rahmenbedingungen, bzw. Faktoren sind für Sie ausschlaggebend beim Konzipieren?

3. What room inside the home do you find most interesting to design?
¿Qué estancia de la vivienda encuentra usted más interesante para diseñar?
Welchen Raum des Hauses finden Sie am spannendsten zu entwerfen?

4. What is your criteria for choosing materials and finishings in a particular room?
¿Cuál es su criterio a la hora de seleccionar los materiales y los acabados en esta estancia?
Welche Kriterien wenden Sie bei der Entscheidung über Materialien und Oberflächen in diesem Raum an?

1. The house of John Soane in London was designed to house his large collection of art and antiquities. The plasticity and ambiguity of the spaces and the manipulation of natural daylight raises the architecture to a spiritual level.

2. The aspirations of the client is the most important aspect of designing a residence. The goal of the designer is to exceed these aspirations and realize space beyond the client's own imagination.

3. The living space is the social hub of all houses and it's relationship to the other spaces is critical. The definition of this space is all encompassing, it can sometimes be the only room in a studio apartment.

4. We are moving away from white minimalist space by using colour and texture more and more in our projects.

1. La casa de John Sloan en Londres fue diseñada para albergar su gran colección de arte y antigüedades. La plasticidad y ambigüedad de los espacios y la manipulación de la luz natural elevan la arquitectura a un grado espiritual.

2. Las expectativas del cliente son el aspecto más importante al diseñar una vivienda. El objetivo del diseñador es sobrepasar esas expectativas y crear un espacio más allá de la imaginación del cliente.

3. El espacio público es el centro social de todas las viviendas y su relación con el resto de espacio es muy importante. La definición de este espacio lo engloba todo; a veces puede ser la única habitación en un apartamento.

4. Nos estamos alejando de los blancos espacios minimalistas al incluir cada vez más el color y la textura en nuestros diseños.

1. Das Haus von John Sloan in London wurde entworfen, um seine große Kunst- und Antiquitätensammlung aufzunehmen. Die Plastizität und Zweideutigkeit der Räume und der Umgang mit dem Tageslicht erhöhen die Architektur auf eine spirituelle Ebene.

2. Die Wünsche des Kunden sind der wichtigste Aspekt beim Entwurf einer Wohnung oder eines Wohnhauses. Ziel des Gestalters ist es, diese Erwartungen noch zu übertreffen und einen Raum zu schaffen, der noch über die Vorstellungskraft des Auftraggebers hinaus geht.

3. Der von allen genutzte Raum ist der soziale Mittelpunkt aller Wohnungen und seine Beziehung zu den übrigen Räumen ist sehr wichtig. Die Definition dieses Raumes bezieht alles mit ein. Manchmal kann es sich dabei um den einzigen Raum in einem Appartement handeln.

4. Wir entfernen uns allmählich von den weißen, minimalistischen Räumen, um im stärkeren Maße wieder Farbe und Textur in unsere Entwürfe einzuführen.

The founders of co-labarchitects have worked for many design firms, on both small and large-scale projects, as design architects and design group leaders before establishing co-labarchitects in 2001. Their design approach focuses on responding positively to the client and to the project's environment in order to materialize the aspirations and potential of each. Co-labarchitects feel that it is important to adapt the needs of the client and at the same time take full advantage of the natural characteristics of each location, finding inspiration from various sources to create proposals based on logical analysis.

Los fundadores de co-labarchitects han trabajado para muchas firmas de diseño, en proyectos de gran y pequeña escala, en calidad de arquitectos diseñadores y jefes de grupo de diseño hasta establecer la firma en 2001. Su enfoque de diseño es el de responder positivamente al cliente y al entorno del proyecto con el objetivo de materializar las aspiraciones y las potencialidades de cada uno. Co-labarchitects considera importante adaptar las necesidades del cliente, y al mismo tiempo explotar las naturaleza de cada lugar, tomando varias fuentes de inspiración para crear propuestas basadas en un análisis lógico.

Die Gründer von co-labarchitects haben bereits für viele Unternehmen im Bereich Innenarchitektur gearbeitet, sowohl in großen als auch in kleinen Projekten. Im Jahre 2001 gründeten sie co-labarchitects. Mit ihren Entwürfen möchten sie die Anforderungen des jeweiligen Kunden und der Umgebung jedes Gebäudes gerecht werden. Für co-labarchitects ist es wichtig, die Bedürfnisse des Kunden zu verstehen und gleichzeitig den Charakter des jeweiligen Ortes als Inspirationsquelle zu nutzen, die man analysiert und als Grundlage der Planung benutzt.

1. What historical reference in particular inspires you when designing a residence?

¿Qué referente histórico en particular le sirve de fuente de inspiración a la hora de proyectar una vivienda?

Welche historische Referenz dient Ihnen als Inspiration beim Entwurf eines Hauses?

2. What is the main factor taken into consideration when designing a residence?

¿Cuál es el principal factor determinante a la hora de diseñar una vivienda?

Welche Rahmenbedingungen, bzw. Faktoren sind für Sie ausschlaggebend beim Konzipieren?

3. What room inside the home do you find most interesting to design?

¿Qué estancia de la vivienda encuentra usted más interesante para diseñar?

Welchen Raum des Hauses finden Sie am spannendsten zu entwerfen?

4. What is your criteria for choosing materials and finishings in a particular room?

¿Cuál es su criterio a la hora de seleccionar los materiales y los acabados en esta estancia?

Welche Kriterien wenden Sie bei der Entscheidung über Materialien und Oberflächen in diesem Raum an?

1. Our goal is appropriateness: for the site, for the client, for the budget. Of course, our primary interest is contemporary architecture, but we often use evocative materials and colors if they are appropriate.

2. We begin the design process by looking at the site, primarily access and lnatural light. With an idea of how best to use the site we then look at the functional organization of the home: flow, adjacencies, program, etc. As the plan begins to develop we start our investigation of the massing and building form.

3. I can't say there is one particular room we find more interesting than others.

4. Our preference is for contemporary design; simple detailing. But we also prefer that our homes be warm and habitable.

1. Nuestro objetivo es la corrección: para el lugar, para el cliente, para el presupuesto. Nuestro interés primordial es la arquitectura contemporánea, claro está, pero a menudo utilizamos materiales y colores evocadores si son apropiados.

2. Empezamos el proceso de diseño observando el solar, principalmente su acceso y la luz que recibe. Con la idea de cómo aprovechar el lugar al máximo, comenzamos a pensar en la organización funcional de la vivienda: la distribución, el programa, etcétera; a medida que se desarrolla el plano, investigamos sobre la forma estructural del edificio.

3. No hay una habitación que nos parezca más interesante que otra.

4. Nuestra preferencia es el diseño moderno, los detalles sencillos, pero nos gusta que nuestras viviendas sean cálidas y habitables.

1. Unser Ziel ist es, dass alles stimmt, für den Standort, für den Kunden, für das Budget. Unser Hauptinteresse gilt der zeitgenössischen Architektur, aber natürlich benutzen wir auch manchmal Materialien und Farben, die auf andere Epochen anspielen, wenn es in den Kontext passt.

2. Wir beginnen die Planung eines Bauvorhabens mit einer Studie des Grundstücks, wobei wir hauptsächlich den Zugang und die Lichtverhältnisse betrachten. So entsteht zunächst eine Idee, wie man den Ort maximal ausnutzen kann. Dann beginnen wir, an die funktionelle Organisation des Wohnhauses zu denken, die Verteilung, die Wohnfunktionen usw.. In dem Maße, in dem der Plan weiter entwickelt wird, fangen wir an, uns über die Form des Gebäudes Gedanken zu machen.

3. Es gibt keinen Raum, den wir interessanter als die übrigen Räume finden.

4. Wir bevorzugen modernes Design mit einfachen Einzelheiten, aber wir möchten warme und wohnliche Räume schaffen.

Donald Billinkoff Architects is an architecture and interior design firm based in New York and founded in 1992. It specializes in the design of residential, commercial, and institutional projects in the New York, New Jersey, Connecticut, and Pennsylvania areas. Their projects, the new construction as well as the renovations, have been featured in many international magazines.

Donald Billinkoff Architects es una firma de arquitectura y diseño interior, con sede en Nueva York y fundada en 1992. Se dedica al diseño de proyectos residenciales, comerciales e institucionales en las zonas de Nueva York, Nueva Jersey, Connecticut y Pensilvania. Se ha destacado su trabajo, dedicado tanto a la obra nueva como a las renovaciones, en numerosas publicaciones internacionales.

Donald Billinkoff Architects ist ein Büro für Architektur und Innenarchitektur in New York, das 1992 gegründet wurde. Hauptsächlich werden hier Wohn- und Geschäftshäuser und Gebäude für Institutionen in den Regionen New York, New Jersey, Connecticut und Pennsylvania geplant. Sowohl die Neu- als auch die Umbauten dieses Architekten wurden in zahlreichen, internationalen Zeitschriften vorgestellt.

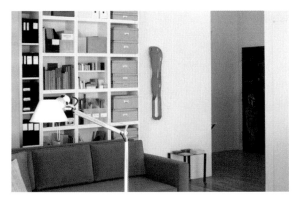

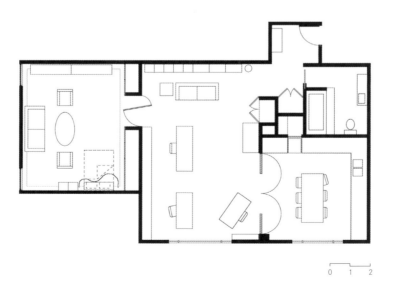

Plan

Planta

Grundriss

1. What historical reference in particular inspires you when designing a residence?

¿Qué referente histórico en particular le sirve de fuente de inspiración a la hora de proyectar una vivienda?

Welche historische Referenz dient Ihnen als Inspiration beim Entwurf eines Hauses?

2. What is the main factor taken into consideration when designing a residence?

¿Cuál es el principal factor determinante a la hora de diseñar una vivienda?

Welche Rahmenbedingungen, bzw. Faktoren sind für Sie ausschlaggebend beim Konzipieren?

3. What room inside the home do you find most interesting to design?

¿Qué estancia de la vivienda encuentra usted más interesante para diseñar?

Welchen Raum des Hauses finden Sie am spannendsten zu entwerfen?

4. What is your criteria for choosing materials and finishings in a particular room?

¿Cuál es su criterio a la hora de seleccionar los materiales y los acabados en esta estancia?

Welche Kriterien wenden Sie bei der Entscheidung über Materialien und Oberflächen in diesem Raum an?

---

1. Case study houses of the forties and fifties as they had open plans, an emphasis on natural light, efficient use of space and the economical use of simple materials.

2. The site, light, views, and natural ventilation are celebrated and maximized whether we are working on an urban loft or a freestanding structure in a rural context.

3. The hub, or the most heavily used space where the family comes together and where they socialize with others. The hub may be the living room, a family room or what is often referred to as the great room where all the social activities overlap.

4. Functionality, beauty, easy of maintenance, texture, durability and we like to introduce clients to materials they may be familiar with used in a new way.

---

1. Las casas típicas de la década de 1940 y 1950 con sus plantas abiertas, el énfasis en la luz natural, el uso eficiente del espacio y la economía en el empleo de los materiales.

2. El lugar, la luz, las vistas y la ventilación natural siempre son destacados en cualquier tipo de proyecto en el que trabajamos, desde un loft urbano hasta una estructura aislada en un entorno rural.

3. El punto neurálgico o el espacio más utilizado donde la familia se suele reunir y se relaciona. Este punto puede ser la sala de estar, una sala familiar o lo que algunas veces se refiere a una gran habitación en donde todas las actividades sociales se integran.

4. Funcionalidad, belleza, fácil mantenimiento, textura, durabilidad y el deseo de mostrar a los clientes una nueva manera de utilizar los materiales.

---

1. Die typischen Häuser aus den Vierziger und Fünfzigerjahren mit ihren offenen Stockwerken, die Bedeutung des Tageslicht, die effiziente Nutzung der Räume und die Sparsamkeit beim Einsatz von Materialien.

2. Der Standort, das Licht, die Aussicht und die natürliche Lüftung sind in jedem unserer Bauvorhaben wichtig. Das gilt sowohl für die Fabriketage in der Stadt als auch für ein einzeln stehendes Gebäude in einer ländlichen Umgebung.

3. Das Zentrum oder der meistbenutzte Raum, in dem sich die Familie trifft oder in dem sie Gäste empfängt. Dieser Ort kann das Wohnzimmer sein, ein Familienzimmer oder manchmal ein großer Raum, in dem sich alle sozialen Aktivitäten überschneiden.

4. Funktionalität, Schönheit, einfache Pflege, Textur, Haltbarkeit und der Wunsch, den Kunden einen neuen Umgang mit den Materialien zu zeigen.

Page Goolrick Architect is an architecture and interior design firm based in New York since 1988. The firm's team operates under the shared belief that design excellence results from a simple, clear, and rational attitude, which will create structures that are suitable for our own time period as well as for each specific context and project. The firm's goal is to be able to simplify everyday functions, and in that way fulfill the varied interests and spatial requirements of each client.

Page Goolrick Architect es una firma de arquitectura y diseño interior con sede en Nueva York desde 1988. El equipo que compone la firma opera en la creencia compartida de que la excelencia en el diseño se logra por medio de una actitud sencilla, clara y racional para crear estructuras adecuadas tanto para nuestro tiempo como para cada programa y contexto específico. El objetivo de la firma es lograr simplificar las funciones diarias y de este modo celebrar la variedad de intereses y las necesidades espaciales de cada cliente.

Page Goolrick Architect ist ein Architekturbüro, das seit 1988 in New York tätig ist. Dieses Architektenteam folgt der Devise, dass man ein ausgezeichnetes Design durch eine einfache, klare und rationale Haltung erreicht, um so Strukturen zu schaffen, die für unsere spezifische Zeit geeignet sind, und zwar für jeden Zweck und Kontext. Ziel des Büros ist es, die täglichen Funktionen zu vereinfachen und so den verschiedenen Interessen jedes Kunden gerecht zu werden und Räume für alle Bedürfnisse zu schaffen.

1. What historical reference in particular inspires you when designing a residence?

¿Qué referente histórico en particular le sirve de fuente de inspiración a la hora de proyectar una vivienda?

Welche historische Referenz dient Ihnen als Inspiration beim Entwurf eines Hauses?

2. What is the main factor taken into consideration when designing a residence?

¿Cuál es el principal factor determinante a la hora de diseñar una vivienda?

Welche Rahmenbedingungen, bzw. Faktoren sind für Sie ausschlaggebend beim Konzipieren?

3. What room inside the home do you find most interesting to design?

¿Qué estancia de la vivienda encuentra usted más interesante para diseñar?

Welchen Raum des Hauses finden Sie am spannendsten zu entwerfen?

4. What is your criteria for choosing materials and finishings in a particular room?

¿Cuál es su criterio a la hora de seleccionar los materiales y los acabados en esta estancia?

Welche Kriterien wenden Sie bei der Entscheidung über Materialien und Oberflächen in diesem Raum an?

1. Our experiences have taught us the importance of local events and microstructures. Especially important to our work is the respect of people's local identity and roots.

2. Architecture is in most cases not the staging of the special, but the design of the common. Like our clothes, buildings must not only fulfil practical, but also emotional requirements. We are not interested in designing just technically perfect buildings that have no 'emotional responders' and therefore feel cold and dead to the user.

3. It's never one room but always the movement between rooms, which creates the space and the emotional experience within it.

4. Materials, finishes and colour are some of the many ingredients of architecture. But we see these ingredients more as an 'enhancer' of conceptions or emotional intentions.

1. Nuestras experiencias nos han enseñado la importancia de las circunstancias concretas y las microestructuras. La identidad de las personas y sus raíces son especialmente importantes en nuestro trabajo.

2. La arquitectura no es, en la mayoría de los casos, el escenario de lo especial, sino el diseño de lo común. Como nuestra ropa, los edificios no sólo deben cumplir requisitos prácticos, sino también emocionales. No estamos interesados en diseñar edificios técnicamente perfectos que no provocan respuestas emocionales y resultan fríos para el habitante.

3. No se trata de una habitación, sino la movilidad entre ellas, que crea un espacio y la experiencia emocional en ellas.

4. Los materiales, los acabados y la gama cromática son algunos de los muchos ingredientes de la arquitectura, pero son elementos que refuerzan los conceptos, no las intenciones emocionales.

1. Unsere Erfahrungen haben uns die Bedeutung punktueller Umstände und von Mikrostrukturen gelehrt. Die Identität von Personen und ihre Wurzeln sind besonders wichtig für unsere Arbeit.

2. Die Architektur ist in den meisten Fällen nicht der Schauplatz des Besonderen, sondern die Gestaltung des Gewöhnlichen. Wie unsere Kleidung sollten auch Gebäude nicht nur praktische Anforderungen erfüllen, sondern auch emotionale. Es interessiert uns nicht, technisch perfekte Gebäude zu entwerfen, die keine Gefühle wach rufen und auf den Benutzer kalt wirken.

3. Es ist nicht ein Raum, sondern die Bewegung zwischen den Räumen, was den Raum und die emotionale Erfahrung innerhalb des Raumes schafft.

4. Die Materialien, Oberflächen und Farben sind nur einige der vielen Zutaten der Architektur, aber sie sind die Elemente, die die emotionalen Konzepte oder Absichten verstärken.

Architects Stefan Camenzind and Michael Grafensteiner, winners of the Young Architect of the Year Award and the International Design Prize, have firmly positioned themselves among the new generation of notable architects. Their work stands out for its fusion of ingenuity and typical Swiss quality. Stefan Camenzind and Michael Grafensteiner founded their own studio in 1995, after having gained experience working in architectural offices in London, Paris, and Los Angeles. At present they have more than 15 architects practicing with them.

Ganadores del premio Joven Arquitecto del Año y el premio de Diseño Internacional, los arquitectos Stefan Camenzind y Michael Grafensteiner forman parte de la nueva generación de arquitectos notables. Su trabajo está influenciado fundamentalmente por una fusión de ingenuidad y calidad típicamente suiza. Después de tener experiencia trabajando en oficinas de arquitectura en Londres, París y Los Ángeles, Stefan Camenzind y Michael Grafensteiner fundaron su propio estudio en 1995 y en la actualidad cuentan con más de 15 arquitectos colaboradores.

Die Architekten Stefan Camenzind und Michael Grafensteiner, Preisträger des Young Architect of the Year-Preises und des International Design Award, gehören mittlerweile zur neuen Generation berühmter Architekten. Ihre Arbeit ist vor allem von der Vermischung von Naivität mit der für die Schweiz so typischen Qualität gekennzeichnet. Nachdem sie bereits für Architekturbüros in London, Paris und Los Angeles gearbeitet hatten, gründeten Stefan Camenzind und Michael Grafensteiner 1995 ihr eigenes Studio, in dem gegenwärtig 15 Architekten zusammenarbeiten.

1. What historical reference in particular inspires you when designing a residence?

¿Qué referente histórico en particular le sirve de fuente de inspiración a la hora de proyectar una vivienda?

Welche historische Referenz dient Ihnen als Inspiration beim Entwurf eines Hauses?

2. What is the main factor taken into consideration when designing a residence?

¿Cuál es el principal factor determinante a la hora de diseñar una vivienda?

Welche Rahmenbedingungen, bzw. Faktoren sind für Sie ausschlaggebend beim Konzipieren?

3. What room inside the home do you find most interesting to design?

¿Qué estancia de la vivienda encuentra usted más interesante para diseñar?

Welchen Raum des Hauses finden Sie am spannendsten zu entwerfen?

4. What is your criteria for choosing materials and finishings in a particular room?

¿Cuál es su criterio a la hora de seleccionar los materiales y los acabados en esta estancia?

Welche Kriterien wenden Sie bei der Entscheidung über Materialien und Oberflächen in diesem Raum an?

1. We are influenced by classic modernist architects and by artists whose work inspires us.

2. The main starting points for us are the existing context, whether it be a loft interior or a wooded site for a house, and the functional needs of the clients. Our goal is to take these given perameters and then transform them into something that transcends the purely functional.

3. What is most important to us is the interconnection of rooms and how one room flows to the next. In terms of individual spaces, we like to design rooms that present specific design challenges and require inventive solutions.

4. We choose our materials based on the character of a particular room. We like to bring color and texture to surfaces through the use of natural materials.

1. Estamos influenciados por los clásicos arquitectos modernos y por artistas cuyo trabajo nos inspira.

2. Los puntos de partida más importantes para nosotros son el entorno, ya sea el interior de un loft o el terreno boscoso para una casa, y las necesidades funcionales de los clientes. Nuestro objetivo es tomar estos parámetros y transformarlos en algo que trascienda lo puramente funcional.

3. Lo que más nos importa es la interconexión entre las estancias y cómo una habitación fluye hacia la siguiente. En términos de espacios individuales, nos gusta diseñar habitaciones que presentan un reto de diseño concreto y requieren soluciones novedosas.

4. Escogemos los materiales según el carácter de una habitación particular. Nos gusta traer color y textura a las superficies con materiales naturales.

1. Wir sind von den klassischen, modernen Architekten und von Künstlern, deren Arbeit uns inspiriert, beeinflusst.

2. Die wichtigsten Ausgangspunkte für uns sind der Kontext, egal, ob es sich um das Innere einer Fabriketage oder ein Waldgrundstück für ein Haus handelt, und die funktionellen Bedürfnisse jedes Kundens. Unser Ziel ist es, diese Parameter zu erkennen und in etwas umzuformen, was das rein Funktionelle übersteigt.

3. Für uns ist die Verbindung zwischen den Räumen, und wie ein Raum zum nächsten hin fließt, am wichtigsten. Was die individuellen Räume betrifft, so genießen wir es, Räume zu gestalten, die eine besondere Herausforderung darstellen und neue Lösungen brauchen.

4. Wir wählen die Materialien entsprechend des Charakters jedes einzelnen Raumes aus. Wir bringen gerne mithilfe von natürlichen Materialien Farbe und Textur auf die Wände.

Roger Hirsch Architect (Roger Hirsch y Miryam Corti) is a design firm that specializes in residential and commercial projects. Over the past twelve years its activities have focused on specific clients and locations, resulting in innovative and functional solutions. The firm has received two awards from the Institute of American Architects (AIA) for its residential and retail store designs.

The interior design firm, Tocar, Inc., consists of Susan Vendar and Christina Sullivan. Their design proposals offer a fresh approach to the concept of elegance, mixing classic and contemporary elements.

Roger Hirsch Architect (Roger Hirsch y Miryam Corti) desarrolla proyectos residenciales y comerciales. En los últimos doce años su trabajo se ha centrado en clientes y emplazamientos concretos que dan como resultado proyectos funcionales e innovadores. La firma ha recibido dos premios del Instituto Americano de Arquitectos (AIA) por sus proyectos de vivienda.

Tocar, Inc., la firma de diseño interior, está compuesta por Susan Vendar y Christina Sullivan. Sus propuestas de diseño ofrecen un acercamiento fresco al concepto de elegancia, mezclando elementos clásicos y contemporáneos.

Roger Hirsch Architect (Roger Hirsch und Miryam Corti) entwirft vor allem Wohn-, Büro- und Geschäftshäuser. In den letzten zwölf Jahren konzentrierte sich das Büro besonders auf funktionelle und innovative Bauten. Dem Büro wurden zwei Preise vom American Institute of Architects (AIA) für seine Wohn- und Geschäftshäuser verliehen.

Tocar, Inc., das Innenarchitekturbüro, wird von Susan Vendar und Christina Sullivan geführt. Ihre Gestaltungsvorschläge nähern sich auf erfrischende Art dem Konzept der Eleganz, indem klassische und zeitgenössische Elemente gemischt werden.

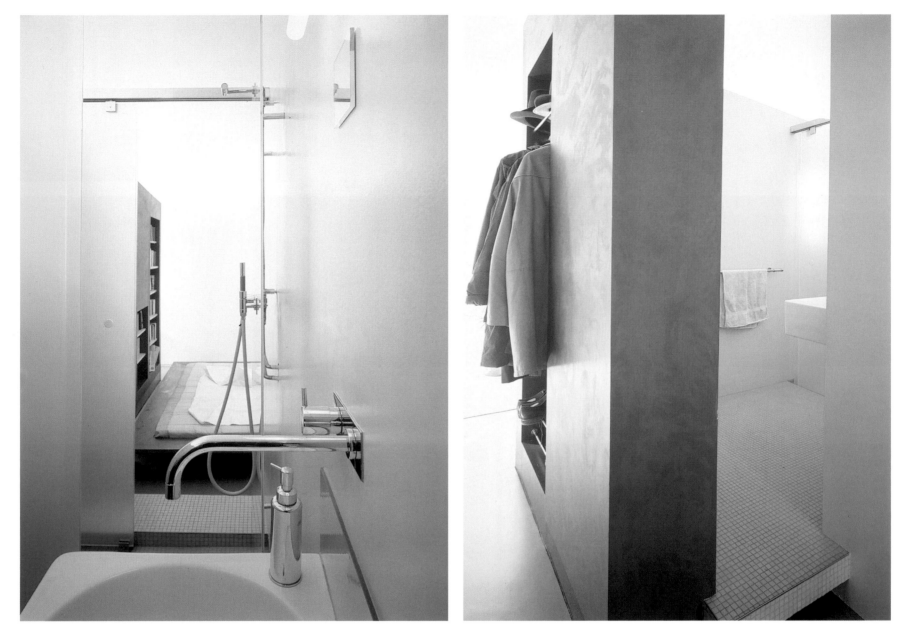

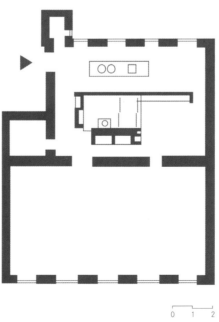

Plan

Planta

Grundriss

0   1   2

1. What historical reference in particular inspires you when designing a residence?
¿Qué referente histórico en particular le sirve de fuente de inspiración a la hora de proyectar una vivienda?
Welche historische Referenz dient Ihnen als Inspiration beim Entwurf eines Hauses?

2. What is the main factor taken into consideration when designing a residence?
¿Cuál es el principal factor determinante a la hora de diseñar una vivienda?
Welche Rahmenbedingungen, bzw. Faktoren sind für Sie ausschlaggebend beim Konzipieren?

3. What room inside the home do you find most interesting to design?
¿Qué estancia de la vivienda encuentra usted más interesante para diseñar?
Welchen Raum des Hauses finden Sie am spannendsten zu entwerfen?

4. What is your criteria for choosing materials and finishings in a particular room?
¿Cuál es su criterio a la hora de seleccionar los materiales y los acabados en esta estancia?
Welche Kriterien wenden Sie bei der Entscheidung über Materialien und Oberflächen in diesem Raum an?

1. Buildings which invite us to use them in a new way: that can be large rooms like lofts in old factories as well as small rooms like the houses of Adolf Loos in Vienna.

2. To give people not only comfort, that is anyway important, but also to make them keen on discovering something new, like children in a barn.

3. It depends on how open the client is, so we are able to change the terms of each room.

4. The effect of materials depends on the way they are used. The unusual combination of well-known materials is often the way to spark people's interest.

1. Los edificios que nos invitan a habitarlos de un modo diferente: pueden ser desde amplios espacios tipo lofts en antiguas fábricas hasta pequeñas habitaciones como en las casas de Adolf Loos en Viena.

2. Ofrecer a la gente no sólo confort, que es importante, sino además despertarles la curiosidad en descubrir algo nuevo, como si fuesen niños en una granja.

3. Depende de cómo sea de abierto el cliente, nosotros seremos capaces de cambiar los términos de cada habitación.

4. El efecto de los materiales depende de la manera en que se utilicen. La combinación inusual de materiales bien conocidos es muchas veces la manera de despertar el interés de la gente.

1. Gebäude, die uns dazu einladen, sie anders zu benutzen, können große Räume im Stile der alter Fabriketagen oder kleine Räume wie in den Häusern von Adolf Loos in Wien sein.

2. Den Menschen soll nicht nur Komfort geboten werden, was sehr wichtig ist, sondern es soll auch eine Neugierde in ihnen geweckt werden, etwas Neues zu entdecken, so wie bei Kindern auf einem Bauernhof.

3. Je nachdem, wie offen der Kunde ist, sind wir dazu in der Lage, die Situation in jedem Raum zu ändern.

4. Die Wirkung der Materialien hängt davon ab, wie sie benutzt werden. Die ungewöhnliche Kombination von gut bekannten Materialien ist oft eine Form, um das Interesse der Menschen zu erwecken.

Mira Thal (Innsbruck, Austria, 1964) and Michael Buchleitner (Stuttgart, Germany, 1959) joined to found the architectural office of Lakonis Architekten in Vienna, in 1995. For them architecture is directly related to man's perception of the natural world, as well as being connected to the makeup of our cultural identity. In this sense, architecture fulfills both functional and economic requirements, by offering universal solutions for our environment.
The firm offers a wide range of services, design, construction management, organization and budget management, in all phases of the project.

Mira Thal (Innsbruck, Austria, 1964) y Michael Buchleitner (Stuttgart, Alemania, 1959) se asociaron y fundaron la oficina de arquitectura Lakonis Architekten en Viena, en 1995. Para ellos la arquitectura está directamente relacionada con nuestra percepción del mundo, de igual modo que está relacionada con la conformación de nuestra identidad cultural. En este sentido la arquitectura da respuestas a exigencias funcionales y económicas para ofrecer soluciones globales a nuestro entorno. La oficina ofrece una gama de servicios, desde el diseño y dirección de obra hasta el control de presupuestos y organización del proyecto.

Mira Thal (Innsbruck, Österreich, 1964) und Michael Buchleitner (Stuttgart, Deutschland, 1959) gründeten im Jahr 1995 in Wien das Architekturbüro Lakonis Architekten. Für die beiden Architekten steht die Architektur in direkter Verbindung mit unserer Wahrnehmung der Welt und der Gestaltung unserer kulturellen Identität. Deshalb gibt die Architektur Antworten auf funktionelle und ökonomische Anforderungen, um globale Lösungen für unsere Umgebung zu bieten. Das Architekturbüro bietet umfassende Dienstleistungen, über Entwurf und Bauleitung bis hin zur Kostenüberwachung, Organisation und Überwachung aller Projektphasen.

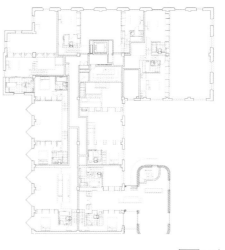

0   3   6

General plans

Plantas generales

Generalgrundrisse

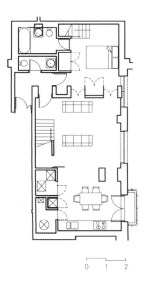

Plan
Planta
Grundriss

Elevations
Alzados
Aufrisse

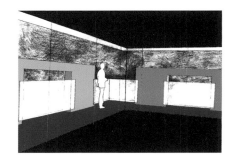

0 1 2

Interior view
Vista interior
Innenaufsicht

Paskin Kyriakides Sands is a London firm founded in 1974 by Douglas Paskin, and it has grown to become a nationally known company thanks to the recognition received for its work. The firm specializes in urban planning, from modest new construction jobs to large urban renewal projects and master plans. Their main emphasis is the integration of the project into its surroundings, and strategic plans. They have vast experience in residential design, from luxury units to large apartment complexes.

Paskin Kyriakides Sands, firma fundada en 1974 en Londres por Douglas Paskin, ha crecido hasta formar una sociedad de fama nacional gracias a los reconocimientos por sus obras. La compañía está especializada en los planos urbanos, desde modestos proyectos de obra nueva hasta grandes reformas urbanas y planos maestros. Destaca la integración de la obra en el entorno y los planos estratégicos. Cuenta con una larga trayectoria en el diseño de residencias, desde unidades de lujo hasta grandes complejos de apartamentos.

Paskin Kyriakides Sands ist ein Unternehmen, das 1974 von Douglas Paskin in London gegründet wurde. Die Firma gewann durch ihre bekannten Projekte internationale Anerkennung. Das Unternehmen hat sich auf Stadtplanung spezialisiert, wobei sowohl Neubauten als auch große Renovierungsprojekte und Masterpläne durchgeführt werden. Die Unternehmensphilosophie basiert auf der Integration der Bauten in ihren Kontext und in die Stadtplanung. Man blickt auf eine langjährige Erfahrung im Bau von Wohnungen und Wohnhäusern zurück, angefangen bei luxuriösen Villen bis hin zu großen Wohnkomplexen.

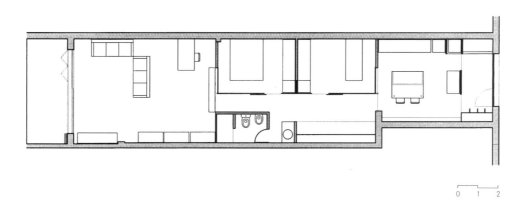

Plan

Planta

Grundriss

1. What historical reference in particular inspires you when designing a residence?
   ¿Qué referente histórico en particular le sirve de fuente de inspiración a la hora de proyectar una vivienda?
   Welche historische Referenz dient Ihnen als Inspiration beim Entwurf eines Hauses?

2. What is the main factor taken into consideration when designing a residence?
   ¿Cuál es el principal factor determinante a la hora de diseñar una vivienda?
   Welche Rahmenbedingungen, bzw. Faktoren sind für Sie ausschlaggebend beim Konzipieren?

3. What room inside the home do you find most interesting to design?
   ¿Qué estancia de la vivienda encuentra usted más interesante para diseñar?
   Welchen Raum des Hauses finden Sie am spannendsten zu entwerfen?

4. What is your criteria for choosing materials and finishings in a particular room?
   ¿Cuál es su criterio a la hora de seleccionar los materiales y los acabados en esta estancia?
   Welche Kriterien wenden Sie bei der Entscheidung über Materialien und Oberflächen in diesem Raum an?

1. It is a cultural reference rather than a historic one. A combination of styles: Colonial, Asian, etc., that we use to create a special environment.

2. Light is a determining factor in the distribution of the rooms. Other important factors are maximizing the space and comfort in each one of them.

3. The kitchen. This is a multifunctional space that the residents enjoy at some time of the day. It has to be a clean, comfortable space, and above all very functional when it comes to fulfilling the customary tasks of this space. It is the inspiration for private or shared enjoyment. The kitchen is where part of life is cooked up.

4. The materials, as well as the space in general, should be functional and easy to clean: steel, glass, marble, wood. Porous materials should never be used.

1. Más que un referente histórico sería de carácter cultural. Una combinación de estilos: colonial, oriental, etcétera, con la que conseguimos un ambiente especial.

2. En la distribución de las estancias, la luz ha sido un factor determinante. También determinantes han sido el conseguir el máximo espacio y confort en cada una de ellas.

3. La cocina. Espacio multifuncional donde en algún momento del día los habitantes disfrutan de ella. Tiene que ser un espacio limpio, cómodo y sobre todo muy funcional a la hora de llevar a cabo las tareas que se desarrollan. La imaginación para el disfrute íntimo o compartido. En la cocina es donde se cuece parte de la vida.

4. Los materiales al igual que el espacio en general deben ser funcionales y de fácil limpieza: acero, cristal, mármol, madera, etcétera. En ningún caso materiales porosos.

1. Ich beziehe mich eher auf einen kulturellen Charakter als auf eine historische Referenz. Eine Kombination aus Stilen, kolonialer, orientalischer Stil, mit denen man eine ganz besondere Atmosphäre schafft.

2. Der wichtigste Faktor für die Verteilung der Räume ist das Licht. Ebenso wichtig ist es, so viel Platz und Bequemlichkeit wie möglich in jedem Raum zu schaffen.

3. Die Küche. Ein multifunktioneller Raum, von dem alle Bewohner irgendwann im Laufe des Tages profitieren. Es muss ein sauberer, bequemer und vor allem funktioneller Ort für die Aufgaben sein, die dort durchgeführt werden. Phantasie, um alleine oder zusammen zu genießen. In der Küche findet ein Teil des Lebens statt.

4. Die Materialien müssen, ebenso wie der Raum selbst, funktionell und leicht zu reinigen sein, Stahl, Glas, Marmor, Holz... Niemals poröse Materialien.

Special Events is an interior design firm founded by Joan Estrada in 1999, in Barcelona. His work mainly focuses, on the interior design of a wide range of projects, from commercial boutiques and shops, to homes, to high-design hotels. Single-family homes are the specialty of this firm, which carries out its work in several Spanish cities. The style is characterized by the purity of the spatial concept and attention to the smallest details.

Special Events es una firma de interiorismo fundada por Joan Estrada en 1999, en Barcelona. Su trabajo se centra principalmente en el diseño interior de una amplia variedad de proyectos, desde boutiques y tiendas comerciales hasta viviendas y hoteles de diseño. Las residencias unifamiliares son la especialidad de esta firma que desarrolla proyectos en varias ciudades españolas. Su estilo se caracteriza por la limpieza en la concepción de los espacios y el cuidado en los mínimos detalles.

Special Events ist ein von Joan Estrada 1999 in Barcelona gegründetes Unternehmen im Bereich Innenarchitektur. Estrada konzentriert sich hauptsächlich auf die Innenarchitektur von sehr verschiedenen Gebäudetypen wie Boutiquen und andere Arten von Geschäftsräumen, Wohnungen und Designhotels. Der Schwerpunkt des Unternehmens liegt in der Gestaltung von Einfamilienhäusern. In mehreren spanischen Städten wurden bereits Aufträge durchgeführt. Typisch für den Stil dieses Innenarchitekten ist die Klarheit der Raumkonzepte und die sorgfältige Ausarbeitung auch der kleinsten Einzelheiten.

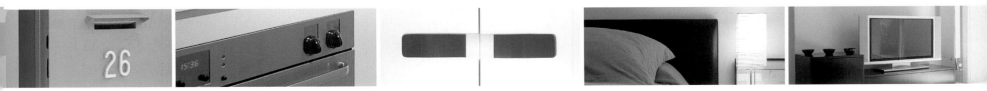

LOFTS

LOFTS / LOFTS

Ling Office and Loft

Light Loft

DeBenedetto / Jiang Loft

TB Guest Loft

Loft in Soho

Frank and Amy Loft

Giobbi / Valentino Residence

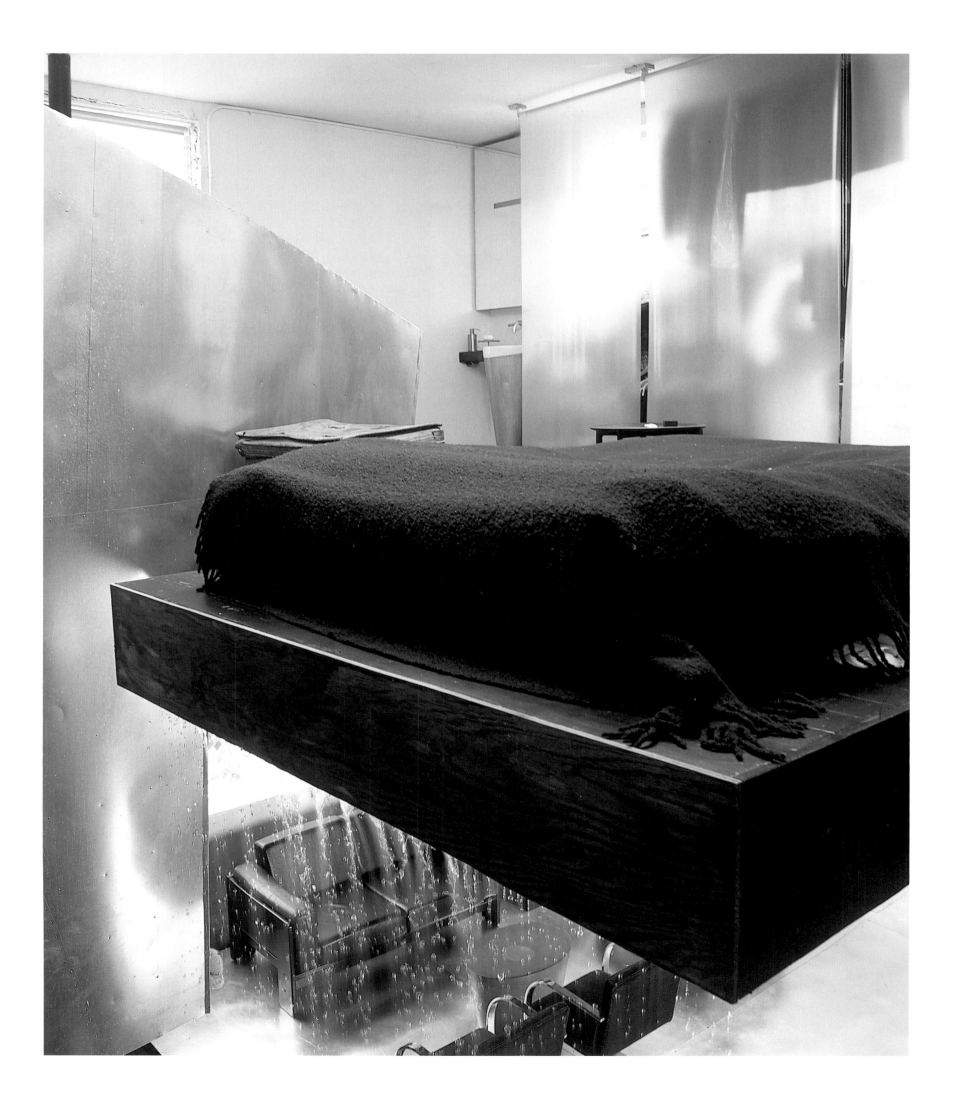

1. What historical reference in particular inspires you when designing a residence?

   ¿Qué referente histórico en particular le sirve de fuente de inspiración a la hora de proyectar una vivienda?

   Welche historische Referenz dient Ihnen als Inspiration beim Entwurf eines Hauses?

2. What is the main factor taken into consideration when designing a residence?

   ¿Cuál es el principal factor determinante a la hora de diseñar una vivienda?

   Welche Rahmenbedingungen, bzw. Faktoren sind für Sie ausschlaggebend beim Konzipieren?

3. What room inside the home do you find most interesting to design?

   ¿Qué estancia de la vivienda encuentra usted más interesante para diseñar?

   Welchen Raum des Hauses finden Sie am spannendsten zu entwerfen?

4. What is your criteria for choosing materials and finishings in a particular room?

   ¿Cuál es su criterio a la hora de seleccionar los materiales y los acabados en esta estancia?

   Welche Kriterien wenden Sie bei der Entscheidung über Materialien und Oberflächen in diesem Raum an?

---

1. Actually I am inspired by sculpture: Richard Serra, Eduardo Chillida, early Giacometti, early Noguchi, Anish Kapoor, Martin Puryear. Among architects I admire early Mies van der Rohe, Le Corbusier, Carlo Scarpa, Pierre Chareau, late Kahn.

2. For me the main factor is the physical idiosyncrasies of the space and the personal idiosyncrasies of the client.

3. I enjoy designing the entertaining space which for me is the kitchen/dining room since I design them together.

4. I like to juxtapose opposite materials and forms. Smooth against hard, rustic against refined.

---

1. Realmente encuentro inspiración en la escultura: Richard Serra, Eduardo Chillida, Anish Kapoor, Martin Puryear o los primeros trabajos de Giacometti y de Noguchi. Entre los arquitectos admiro las primeras obras de Mies van der Rohe, Le Corbusier, Carlo Scarpa, Pierre Chareau y las últimas obras de Kahn.

2. El principal factor es la idiosincrasia del espacio y la propia personalidad de cada cliente.

3. Disfruto diseñando un espacio divertido como es la cocina y comedor, ya que los diseño conjuntamente.

4. Me gusta la yuxtaposición de formas y materiales opuestos. Suave contra fuerte, rústico en oposición a refinado.

---

1. Ich werde wirklich von der Bildhauerei inspiriert. Richard Serra, Eduardo Chillida, Anish Kapoor, Martin Puryear oder die ersten Arbeiten von Giacometti und Noguchi. Unter den Architekten bin ich ein Bewunderer der ersten Werke von Mies van der Rohe, Le Corbusier, Carlo Scarpa, Pierre Chareau und der letzten Bauten von Kahn.

2. Der wichtigste Faktor ist die Idiosynkrasie des Raumes und die eigene, persönliche jedes Kundens.

3. Ich genieße es, unterhaltsame Räume wie die Küche und das Speisezimmer zu entwerfen, die ich beide zusammen entwerfe.

4. Ich liebe die Nebeneinanderstellung von gegensätzlichen Formen und Farben. Weich gegen stark, rustikal gegen elegant.

David Ling's multicultural background strongly influences his professional career. Brought up in the United States and educated in Europe, Ling still maintains his ties with China. After working as an associate in the offices of Richard Meier and I. M. Pei he established his own architectural office, David Ling Architects, in 1992. Ling defines the essence of his work as an artistic integration of space, form, light, and function enriched with materials. For Ling, all projects present a unique challenge, because of their diverse natures and variety of locations.

La formación multicultural de David Ling influyó en su carrera profesional. Creció en Estados Unidos y recibió su educación en Europa, pero nunca rompió con sus raíces chinas. Después de trabajar como colaborador asociado en las oficinas de Richard Meier e I. M. Pei, estableció su propia oficina de arquitectura, David Ling Architects, en 1992. La esencia de su obra la define él mismo como una integración artística entre espacio, forma, luz y función enriquecida con materialidad. Ling trata proyectos y lugares muy diversos de manera individual.

Die berufliche Laufbahn von David Ling ist erheblich durch seine multikulturelle Erziehung geprägt. Er wuchs in den Vereinigten Staaten auf, erhielt seine Ausbildung in Europa und ist durch seine Herkunft für immer mit China verbunden. Nachdem er als assoziierter Mitarbeiter im Büro von Richard Meier und I. M. Pei tätig war, gründete er 1992 sein eigenes Architekturbüro David Ling Architects. Er selbst definiert das Wesentliche seiner Arbeit als eine künstlerische Integration von Raum, Form, Licht und Funktion, die durch Gegenständlichkeit bereichert wird. Ling beschäftigt sich mit sehr verschiedenen Projekten und Standorten.

Desai / Chia Architecture was founded in 1995 by Catherine Chia and Arjun Desai in New York City. The architectural style of the firm is based on simplicity and an emphasis on the careful and articulated use of light and materials. Special attention is given to the roles of space and form in the design and function of each project. The firm is not given to excessive conceptualization; rather, it sees architecture as a field where tradition, innovation, and imagination should be present in proper measure.

Desai / Chia Architecture fue establecida en 1995 por Catherine Chia y Arjun Desai en la ciudad de Nueva York. La firma se centra en una arquitectura que busca la simplicidad con un énfasis en el uso cuidadoso y articulado de la uz y los materiales. El espacio y la forma están enlazados a una consideración detenida del programa y la función de cada proyecto. La firma no se esfuerza por un camino de excesiva conceptualidad, sino que entiende la arquitectura como un oficio en donde la tradición, la innovación y la imaginación deben estar presentes en su justa medida.

Desai / Chia Architecture wurde 1995 von Catherine Chia und Arjun Desai in New York gegründet. Das Unternehmen sucht mit seiner Architektur die Einfachheit, wobei besonderer Nachdruck auf den intelligenten Gebrauch des Lichtes und der Materialien gelegt wird. Bei allen Wohnfunktionen und auch der Gesamtfunktion jedes einzelnen Gebäudes werden Form und Raum berücksichtigt. Das Unternehmen versucht, nicht den Weg der übertriebenen Konzeptualität einzuschlagen, sondern seine Architektur als ein Handwerk aufzufassen, in dem die Tradition, die Innovation und die Phantasie in der richtigen Menge vorhanden sind.

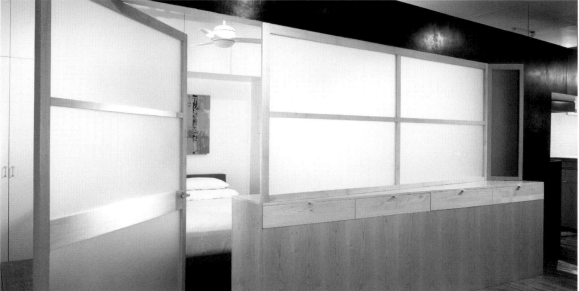

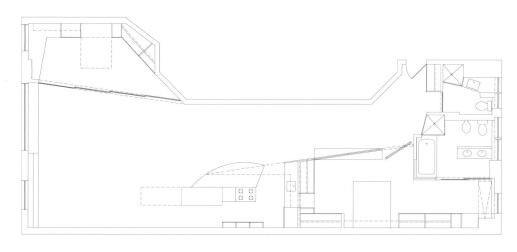

Plan

Planta

Grundriss

0   1   2

1. What historical reference in particular inspires you when designing a residence?

¿Qué referente histórico en particular le sirve de fuente de inspiración a la hora de proyectar una vivienda?

Welche historische Referenz dient Ihnen als Inspiration beim Entwurf eines Hauses?

2. What is the main factor taken into consideration when designing a residence?

¿Cuál es el principal factor determinante a la hora de diseñar una vivienda?

Welche Rahmenbedingungen, bzw. Faktoren sind für Sie ausschlaggebend beim Konzipieren?

3. What room inside the home do you find most interesting to design?

¿Qué estancia de la vivienda encuentra usted más interesante para diseñar?

Welchen Raum des Hauses finden Sie am spannendsten zu entwerfen?

4. What is your criteria for choosing materials and finishings in a particular room?

¿Cuál es su criterio a la hora de seleccionar los materiales y los acabados en esta estancia?

Welche Kriterien wenden Sie bei der Entscheidung über Materialien und Oberflächen in diesem Raum an?

---

1. We try to bring the sum of our travels and experience to each projects; also the particular local history and the vernacular are important to us. One of our recurring favorite historical references is Fatepur Sikra in Rajasthan, India. It seems relevant to all scales and types of projects.

2. Interpreting a client's program is the first creative step in a design. We then think of these ideas in relationship to the specific site.

3. Those spaces that share multiple functions as well as connector spaces between specific rooms.

4. Light and continuity.

---

1. Intentamos volcar la suma de nuestros viajes y experiencias en cada proyecto; asimismo, la historia particular y lo vernacular es importante para nosotros. Una de nuestras referencias históricas favoritas más recurrentes es Fatepur Sikra, en Rajastán, India. Parece relevante a cualquier escala y tipo de proyecto.

2. Interpretar los requerimientos del cliente es el primer paso creativo en el diseño. Es cuando entonces pensamos en estas ideas en relación con el lugar específico.

3. Aquellos espacios que comparten múltiples funciones así como los espacios conectores entre habitaciones determinadas.

4. La luz y la continuidad.

---

1. Wir versuchen, die Summe unserer Reisen und Erfahrungen in jede Planung einzubringen. Ebenso wichtig ist für uns die jeweilige Geschichte und volkstümliche Kultur. Eine unserer liebsten historischen Referenzen ist Fatepur Sikra, in Rajasthan in Indien. Sie scheint für jede Art und Größenordnung der Planung eine Rolle zu spielen.

2. Der erste kreative Schritt für die Gestaltung ist die Interpretation der Bedürfnisse des Kunden. Anschließend denken wir an diese Ideen im Zusammenhang mit dem spezifischen Standort.

3. Die Räume, die mehreren Funktionen dienen und die Räume, die verschiedene Zimmer miteinander verbinden.

4. Das Licht und die Kontinuität.

Smith and Thompson Architects is an architectural firm that was founded by G. Phillip Smith and Douglas Thompson in 1975 in New York. The office mainly designs residences, institutions, and commercial interiors. In 1989 they won a competition to do the construction of the East Hampton airport. They earned the Beaux Arch award for the design of the Kleeb residence, and the AIA Award for the design of the Jacques Marchais Tibetan Art Museum.

Smith and Thompson Architects es una firma de arquitectura fundada por G. Phillip Smith y Douglas Thompson en 1975 en Nueva York. La oficina desarrolla principalmente proyectos de vivienda, instituciones e interiores comerciales. En 1989 fue seleccionada gracias a un concurso para construir el aeropuerto de East Hampton y ha sido galardonada con premios como el Beaux Arch Award, por el diseño de la Residencia Kleeb, y el AIA Award, por el diseño de Museo de Arte Tibetano Jacques Marchais.

Smith and Thompson Architects wurde 1975 von G. Phillip Smith und Douglas Thompson in New York gegründet. Das Unternehmen plant hauptsächlich Wohnungen und Wohnhäuser, Gebäude für Institutionen und Geschäftsräume. 1989 gewann es die Ausschreibung für die Errichtung des Flughafens von East Hampton und ihm wurden mehrere Preise wie der Beaux Arch Award für die Gestaltung des Wohnhauses Kleeb und der AIA Award für die Gestaltung des Museum for Tibetan Art Jacques Marchais verliehen.

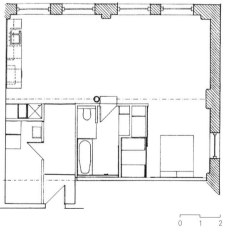

Plan
Planta
Grundriss

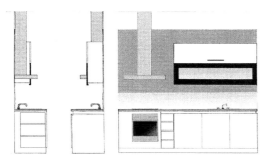

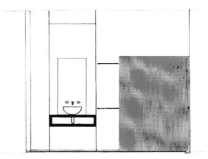

Interior elevations

Alzados interiores

Innenansicht

1. What historical reference in particular inspires you when designing a residence?
   ¿Qué referente histórico en particular le sirve de fuente de inspiración a la hora de proyectar una vivienda?
   Welche historische Referenz dient Ihnen als Inspiration beim Entwurf eines Hauses?

2. What is the main factor taken into consideration when designing a residence?
   ¿Cuál es el principal factor determinante a la hora de diseñar una vivienda?
   Welche Rahmenbedingungen, bzw. Faktoren sind für Sie ausschlaggebend beim Konzipieren?

3. What room inside the home do you find most interesting to design?
   ¿Qué estancia de la vivienda encuentra usted más interesante para diseñar?
   Welchen Raum des Hauses finden Sie am spannendsten zu entwerfen?

4. What is your criteria for choosing materials and finishings in a particular room?
   ¿Cuál es su criterio a la hora de seleccionar los materiales y los acabados en esta estancia?
   Welche Kriterien wenden Sie bei der Entscheidung über Materialien und Oberflächen in diesem Raum an?

1. There is no historic reference in particular however I employ a modernist design sensibility.

2. The main factor taken into consideration when designing a residence is respect to the original environment and pared back design where every single room is ergonomic, energy efficient and aesthetically beautiful to be in.

3. The bathroom.

4. A minimal and natural colour palette which mirrors finishes throughout the interior. In this case bluestone.

1. Ninguna referencia histórica en particular, aunque utilizo un enfoque del diseño modernista.

2. El factor más importante que tener en cuenta al diseñar una vivienda es el respeto por el entorno original y la creación de un diseño mínimo en el cual todas las habitaciones sean ergonómicas, energéticamente eficiente y estéticamente agradable.

3. El baño.

4. Una gama de colores mínima y natural que refleje los acabados en todo el interior.

1. Keine historische Referenz im Besonderen, obwohl ich mich auf das Konzept des modernistischen Designs beziehe.

2. Der wichtigste Faktor, der beim Entwurf einer Wohnung oder eines Hauses beachtet werden muss, ist der Respekt für die ursprüngliche Umgebung und die Schaffung eines minimalen Designs, in dem alle Räume ergonomisch, energetisch wirksam und ästhetisch angenehm sind.

3. Das Bad.

4. Eine minimale und natürliche Farbpalette, die Gestaltungselemente im ganzen Inneren unterstreicht.

The philosophy of the Tom McCallum design firm is to condense the practice into an essential search for beauty, ergonomics, and energy efficiency. To achieve a design that flows harmoniously, a systematic method is employed in every project, first analyzing the characteristics of the site, and later introducing the functional aspects. The design is always conditioned more by the ergonomic solutions for the use of the space than by decisions based on esthetics. Natural colors complement this Minimalist approach. This results in interiors that look spacious, that are easy to use, pleasing to touch, and visually calm.

La filosofía de la firma de diseño Tom McCallum es la de condensar la práctica en una búsqueda esencial de lo bello, ergonómico y energéticamente eficiente. Para lograr un diseño que fluye armónicamente los proyectos son abordados mediante un método en donde se analizan primero las características del lugar para luego introducir la funcionalidad. El diseño está condicionado más por soluciones ergonómicas de uso que por decisiones estéticas. Los colores naturales complementan esta ética minimalista. En consecuencia, se obtienen interiores prácticos, perceptiblemente amplios, atractivos al tacto y visualmente tranquilos.

Die Philosophie des Designbüros Tom McCallum verbindet die Aspekte Schönheit, Ergonomie und Ökonomie. Für die harmonische Gestaltung ihrer jeweiligen Projekte werden zunächst die Umstände jedes Ortes systematisch analysiert, dann werden die funktionellen Aspekte eingeführt. Deshalb unterliegt die Gestaltung immer den ergonomischen Aspekten der Benutzung des Ortes, aber sie basiert auch auf ästhetischen Gesichtspunkten. Natürliche Farben ergänzen das minimalistische Design. So entstehen leicht zu nutzende Räume, die weiträumig wirken, einladend sind und eine visuelle Ruhe ausstrahlen.

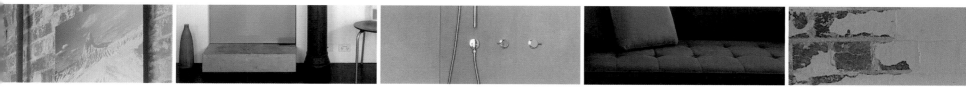

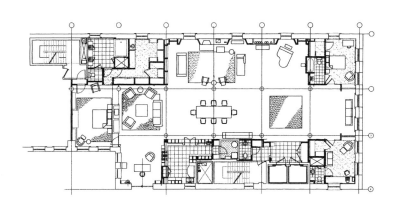

0 2 4

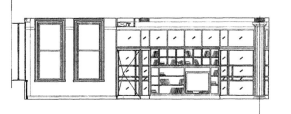

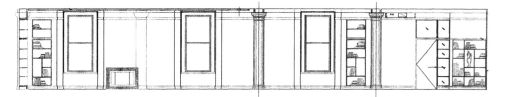

Plan
Planta
Grundriss

Sections
Secciones
Schnitte

Sections

Secciones

Schnitte

1. What historical reference in particular inspires you when designing a residence?

¿Qué referente histórico en particular le sirve de fuente de inspiración a la hora de proyectar una vivienda?

Welche historische Referenz dient Ihnen als Inspiration beim Entwurf eines Hauses?

2. What is the main factor taken into consideration when designing a residence?

¿Cuál es el principal factor determinante a la hora de diseñar una vivienda?

Welche Rahmenbedingungen, bzw. Faktoren sind für Sie ausschlaggebend beim Konzipieren?

3. What room inside the home do you find most interesting to design?

¿Qué estancia de la vivienda encuentra usted más interesante para diseñar?

Welchen Raum des Hauses finden Sie am spannendsten zu entwerfen?

4. What is your criteria for choosing materials and finishings in a particular room?

¿Cuál es su criterio a la hora de seleccionar los materiales y los acabados en esta estancia?

Welche Kriterien wenden Sie bei der Entscheidung über Materialien und Oberflächen in diesem Raum an?

---

1. [Z. Khalili]: My inspirations are the twentieth century, in particular the works of Le Corbusier, Louis Kahn and Ludwig Mies van der Rohe.
[A. Neratoff]: The Baroque in France during the 18th century, when a rarely innovation in small scale domestic architecture happened.

2. [Z. Khalili]: Different approaches to designing a house might be taken, nevetheless the relationship of a house to site remains the main generator of form.
[A. Neratoff]: The cultural framework, the clients' needs and cultural references, etc.

3. [Z. Khalili]: Any room, which has a mixed used function.
[A. Neratoff]: Any room that does not work out right away.

4. [Z. Khalili]: They are based on the design concept, function of the room, client preferences and creating a particular mood.
[A. Neratoff]: Their ability to define the shape of the three-dimensional forms they clad.

---

1. [Z. Khalili]: Mi fuente de inspiración es el siglo XX, en particular los trabajos de Le Corbusier, Louis Kahn y Ludwig Mies van der Rohe.
[A. Neratoff]: El barroco francés durante el siglo XVIII, donde hubo una peculiar innovación en la arquitectura doméstica a pequeña escala.

2. [Z. Khalili]: Se puede abordar de diferentes maneras; sin embargo, la relación entre la casa y el lugar sigue siendo el principal generador de la forma.
[A. Neratoff]: El marco cultural, las necesidades del cliente, las referencias culturales, etcétera.

3. [Z. Khalili]: Cualquier habitación que tenga un uso mixto.
[A. Neratoff]: Cualquier habitación que no se entienda como tal.

4. [Z. Khalili]: Están basados en el concepto de diseño, la función de la habitación, las preferencias del cliente y el generar un estado de ánimo particular.
[A. Neratoff]: La habilidad de los materiales para moldear la forma tridimensional que reviste.

---

1. [Z. Khalili]: Meine Inspirationsquelle ist das 20. Jahrhundert, insbesondere die Arbeiten von Le Corbusier, Louis Kahn und Ludwig Mies van der Rohe.
[A. Neratoff]: Der französische Barock im 18. Jahrhundert, wo es zu einer bedeutenden Innovation in der Architektur von kleineren Wohnhäusern kam.

2. [Z. Khalili]: Man kann an die Gestaltung eines Hauses auf verschiedene Weisen herangehen. Jedoch ist die Beziehung zwischen dem Haus und dem Ort der wichtigste Faktor für die Form.
[A. Neratoff]: Die kulturellen Rahmenbedingungen, die Ansprüche des Kunden, kulturelle Referenzen...

3. [Z. Khalili]: Jegliches Zimmer mit gemischter Nutzung.
[A. Neratoff]: Jeglicher Raum, der nicht als solcher verstanden wird.

4. [Z. Khalili]: Es basiert auf dem Konzept der Gestaltung, der Funktion des Raumes, den Vorlieben des Kundens und auf dem Hervorrufen eines besonderen Gemütszustandes.
[A. Neratoff]: Die Fähigkeit der Materialien, eine dreidimensionale Form zu schaffen, die sie verkleiden.

The Iranian architect Ziba Khalili grew up in Iran and pursued her professional education in France. After receiving a Master of Architecture degree she worked in Paris as an architect for several years. In 1986 she moved to New York where she studied sculpture, winning several prizes for her work. She founded her own architectural firm in 1990 and completed projects in New York and Paris.

Alexandr Neratoff is a native of New York and grew up in the community of Russian immigrants that was formed after the Russian revolution. He received his professional education in the United States.

La arquitecta iraní Ziba Khalili creció en Irán y recibió su educación profesional en Francia. Después de adquirir un máster en Arquitectura trabajó en París como arquitecta durante varios años. En 1986 se trasladó a Nueva York en donde complementó sus estudios en escultura y ganó varios premios por su trabajo. Fundó su propia firma de arquitectura en 1990 y ha desarrollado proyectos en Nueva York y París. Alexandr Neratoff es original de Nueva York y creció dentro de la comunidad de inmigrantes rusos instalados después de la revolución rusa. Su educación profesional la recibió en Estados Unidos.

Die aus dem Iran stammende und dort aufgewachsene Architektin Ziba Khalili absolvierte ihr Studium in Frankreich. Nach dem Studium arbeitete sie mehrere Jahre als Architektin in Paris. 1986 zog sie nach New York um, um sich als Bildhauerin weiterzubilden. Sie gewann mehrere Preise für ihre bildhauerischen Arbeiten. 1990 gründete sie ihr eigenes Architekturbüro und ist seitdem in New York und Paris tätig. Alexandr Neratoff stammt aus New York und wuchs in der Gemeinschaft der russischen Emigranten nach der russischen Revolution auf. Er besuchte die Schule in Frankreich und absolvierte sein Studium in den USA.

This project was designed for a New York couple — one an art critic and the other a movie editor — living in the Hell's Kitchen neighborhood. The residence occupies an entire floor of an old industrial building, and has panoramic views of the city on three sides. The design highlights the industrial context, positioning new elements as if they were sculptures to complement the space and define the layout of the apartment. The result is a box, in which functions like the kitchen and the support areas are consolidated, defining the public and private areas of the loft. The oversize sliding doors that can be opened completely to integrate these areas with the rest of the space are an important element of the design. In general, the color white, the original polished concrete floors, and the exposed utility installations are the predominant elements that emphasize the character of the space. A collection of furniture and decorative elements in wood and soft textiles act as a contrast and create a comfortable environment.

Frank and Amy Loft

Resolution: 4 architecture

New York, NY, USA, 2000
Photos © Reto Guntli / zapaimages

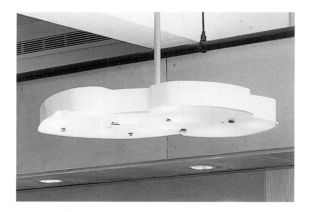

Este proyecto fue diseñado para una pareja, un crítico de arte y un editor de cine en el barrio de Hell's Kitchen de Nueva York. La vivienda se ubica en un antiguo edificio industrial, ocupa la totalidad de la planta de la estructura y cuenta con panorámicas urbanas extensas en tres de sus lados. El diseño realza el contexto industrial colocando elementos nuevos, de forma escultórica, que complementan el espacio existente y solucionan el programa de

Dieser Wohnraum wurde für ein Paar, Kunstkritiker und Cutterin, im Viertel Hell's Kitchen in New York geschaffen. Die Wohnung liegt in einem ehemaligen Industriegebäude und nimmt ein gesamtes Stockwerk ein. Von ihr aus hat man einen wundervollen Blick auf die Stadtlandschaft auf drei Seiten. Die Gestaltung unterstreicht den industriellen Kontext und bringt neue, skulpturelle Elemente ein, die den bereits existierenden Raum ergänzen und Lösungen

la vivienda. El resultado es una caja en donde se condensan los servicios, como la cocina y las zonas de apoyo, y define la esfera pública y privada del loft. Un elemento primordial de esta caja son las puertas correderas de gran formato que se pueden abrir completamente e integrar estas zonas al resto del espacio. En general, predomina el blanco, el hormigón pulido original del suelo, las ventanas existentes y las instalaciones a la vista; elementos que acentúan el carácter industrial del espacio. Como contrapunto, una colección de muebles y elementos decorativos de madera y suaves tejidos dan calidez y crean un entorno acogedor.

für die Wohnfunktionen schaffen. Als Ergebnis entstand eine Kiste, in der sich die funktionellen Zonen wie die Küche und zusätzlichen Räume konzentrieren, und die die öffentlich und privat genutzten Bereiche des Loftes definiert. Ein wichtiges Element dieser Kiste sind die großen Schiebetüren, die völlig geöffnet werden können, um diese Bereiche in den übrigen Raum zu integrieren. Die im allgemeinen vorherrschende Farbe ist weiß, außerdem wurden die originalen, polierten Betonfußböden, die Fenster und die nicht unter Putz liegenden Installationen beibehalten, was den industriellen Charakter des Raumes unterstreicht. Als Kontrapunkt dient eine Sammlung von dekorativen Möbeln und Elementen aus Holz und weich wirkende Stoffe, die die Räume warm und einladend wirken lassen.

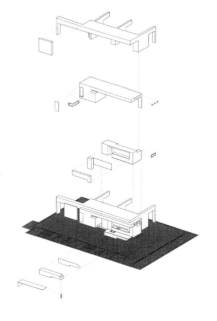

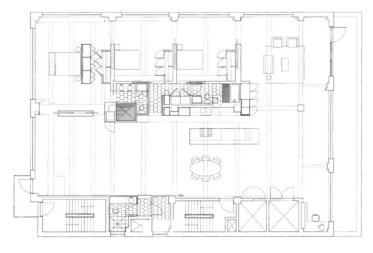

0 2 4

Plan

Planta

Grundriss

Axonometry

Axonometría

Axonometrie

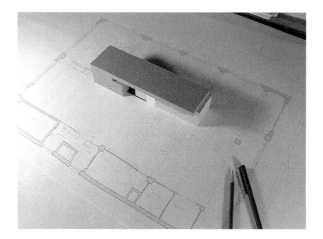

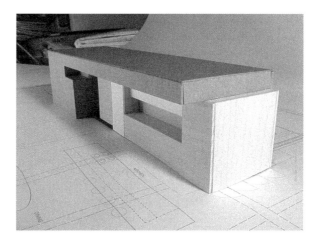

Model

Modelo

Modell

Resolution: 4 architecture is an architectural firm that was founded in 1990 in New York by Joseph Tanney and Robert Luntz. At the present time the company has a team of 10 people who have completed many projects of every size. Their work has earned them several awards including the AIA Award for the design of the offices of an Internet service provider, and a home for the architect Peter Eisenman, as well as the first place award in a contest to design a prefabricated house in Pittsboro.

Resolution: 4 architecture es una firma de arquitectura fundada en 1990 en Nueva York y compuesta por Joseph Tanney y Robert Luntz. Actualmente se compone de diez personas y ha completado una gran variedad de proyectos a diferentes escalas. Su obra ha sido merecedora de varios premios incluyendo los AIA Awards por el diseño de una oficina de servicios de internet, una residencia para el arquitecto Peter Eisenman y ganadores del concurso para el diseño de una casa prefabricada en Pittsboro.

Resolution: 4 architecture ist ein Architekturbüro, das 1990 von Joseph Tanney und Robert Luntz in New York gegründet wurde. Im Augenblick beschäftigt das Unternehmen 10 feste Mitarbeiter und hat bereits zahlreiche Projekte verschiedener Größenordnung durchgeführt. Dem Unternehmen wurden bereits mehrere Preise verliehen, darunter die AIA Awards für die Gestaltung eines Büros für Internetdienstleistungen, ein Preis für ein Wohnhaus für den Architekten Peter Eisenmann und den ersten Platz in einem Wettbewerb für ein Fertighaus in Pittsboro, NC.

0 1 2

Plan
Planta
Grundriss

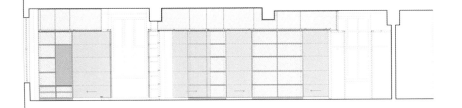

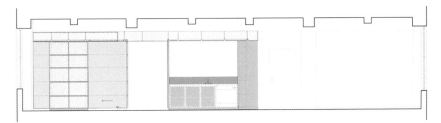

Transversal sections

Secciones transversales

Querschnitt

Kevin Bone and Joseph Levine established their own architecture studio in 1982, with the premise that New York City's constructed environment presents special opportunities, as well as particular problems, for small architecture firms. The firm takes special interest in the materials and construction details that they introduce into their work. The projects strive to be simple, modern, and well constructed, with unexpected combinations of materials and sensitive detailing in their assembly.

Kevin Bone y Joseph Levine establecieron su propio estudio de arquitectura en 1982. Partieron de su creencia que el entorno construido de la ciudad de Nueva York presenta oportunidades especiales, así como problemas particulares para las pequeñas firmas de arquitectura. El trabajo de esta empresa toma interés en los materiales y los detalles constructivos para introducirlos en sus encargos. Obras que pretenden ser simples, modernas, bien construidas, con inesperadas combinaciones de materiales y empleando detalles sensibles en su elaboración.

Kevin Bone und Joseph Levine eröffneten ihr eigenes Architekturbüro 1982. Sie waren davon überzeugt, dass sich in der Umgebung von New York für kleine Architekturunternehmen interessante Möglichkeiten ergeben würden, und ganz besondere Probleme zu lösen wären. Die Firma brachte vor allem ihr Interesse an den Materialien und baulichen Details in ihre Arbeit ein. Es wurden einfache, moderne und hochwertige Gebäude errichtet, mit überraschenden Materialkombinationen und interessanten Einzelheiten.

Directory

Directorio

Direktorium

Christoff:Finio architecture
250 West Broadway, 4th floor,
New York, NY 10013, USA
T: +1 212 219 1026
F: +1 212 219 9165
www.christofffinio.com

co-labarchitects
24/28A Hatton Wall,
London EC1N 8JH, UK
T +44 207 242 7255
F +44 207 242 7266
architecture@co-lab.net
www.co-lab.net

Alden Maddry Architect
928 Lorimer Street, Brooklyn, New York,
NY 11222, USA
T: +1 718 383 1947
am@aldenmaddry.com
www.aldenmaddry.com

Basil Walter Architects
611 Broadway, Suite 311, New York,
NY 10012, USA
T: +1 212 505 1955
F: +1 212 475 7320

Bone / Levine Architects
561 Broadway, 8D, New York,
NY 10012, USA
T: +1 212 219 1038
F: +1 212 226 8056
www.bonelevine.net

Callas Shortridge Architects
3621 Hayden Avenue, Culver City,
CA 90232, USA
T: +1 310 280 0404
F: +1 310 280 0414
mail@callas-shortridge.com
www.callas-shortridge.com

Camenzind Evolution
Samariterstrasse 5, Postfach,
Zurich 8030, Switzerland
T: +41 44 253 9500
F: +41 44 253 9510
info@CamenzindEvolution.com
www.CamenzindEvolution.com

Daniele Claudio Taddei
Feldeggstrasse 54, Zurich 8008,
Switzerland
T: +41 79 409 48 50
taddei@milnor.net

David Ling
225 East 21st Street, New York,
NY 10010, USA
T: +1 212 982 7089
F: +1 212 475 1336
www.davidlingarchitect.com

Delugan_Meissl
Mittersteig 13/4, Vienna 1040, Austria
T: +43 1 585 36 90
F: +43 1 585 36 90-11
haasler@deluganmeissl.at
www.deluganmeissl.at

Desai / Chia Architecture
54 West 21st Street, New York,
NY 10010, USA
T: +1 212 366 9630
F: +1 212 366 9278
www.desaichia.com

Donald Billinkoff Architects
310 Riverside Drive 202-1, New York,
NY 10025, USA
T: +1 212 678 7755
F: +1 212 678 7743
yprokesch@billinkoff.com
www.billinkoff.com

Fung + Blatt Architects
104 N. Avenue 56, Suite 3A, Los Angeles,
CA 90042, USA
T: +1 323 255 8368
F: +1 323 255 3646
contact@fungandblatt.com
www.fungandblatt.com

Gabellini Associates
665 Broadway, Suite 706, New York,
NY 10012, USA
T: +1 212 388 1700
F: +1 212 388 1808
www.gabelliniassociates.com

Gregory Phillips Architects
66 Great Cumberland Place,
London W1H 7FD, UK
T: +44 207 724 3040
www.gregoryphillips.com

Guillermo Arias + Luis Cuartas
Carrera 11 84-42, int. 5, Bogotá,
Colombia
T: +57 1 257 9501
garias@octubre.com.co
www.octubre.com.co

Holodeck.at
Friedrichstrasse 6/15,
Vienna 1010, Austria
T: +43 1 524 8133-0
F: +43 1 524 8133-4
vienna@holodeck.at
www.holodeck.at

Insite Architecture Design
20 Rue de Billancourt,
Boulogne 92100, France
T: +33 01 41 10 22 70
F: +33 01 41 10 22 71
www.insitedsign.com

Joan Estrada / Special Events
Vigatans 6, bajos, Barcelona 08003, Spain
T: +34 93 268 8614
F: +34 93 268 8615
joanestrada@joanestrada.com
www.joanestrada.com

John Wardle Architects
Level 10, 180 Rusell Street, Melbourne,
Victoria 3000, Australia
T: +61 3 9654 8700
F: +61 3 6954 8755
johnwardle@johnwardlearchitects.com
www. johnwardlearchitects.com

Jonathan Levi Architects
266 Beacon Street, Boston,
MA 02116, USA
T: +1 617 437 9458
www.leviarc.com

Lakonis Architekten
Rueppgasse 11, Vienna 1020, Austria
T: +43 1 216 0 215
buchleitner.thal@lakonis.at
www.lakonis.at

Leo Frei Architekten
Bergstrasse 50, Stäfa 8712, Switzerland
T: +41 1 926 7401
info@frei-arch.ch
www.frei-arch.ch

Marcio Kogan
Al Tiete, 505, São Paulo, Brasil
T: +55 011 3018 3522
F: +55 011 3063 3424
mk-mk@uol.com.br

Mark Mack Architects
2343 Eastern Court
Venice, CA 90291, USA
T: +1 310 822 0094
F: +1 310 822 0019
office@markmack.com
www.markmack.com

Page Goolrick Architect
20 W 22 Street, Suite 1505, New York,
NY 10010, USA
T: +1 212 219 3666
F: +1 212 414 5768
pg@goolrick.com
www.goolrick.com

Paskin Kyriakides Sands
7 Cliff Road Studios, London NW1 9AN, UK
T: +44 207 424 4800
F: +44 207 424 4801
info@pksarchitects.com
www.pksarchitects.com

Resolution: 4 architecture
150 W, 28th Street, Suite 1902, New York,
NY 10001, USA
T: +1 212 675 9266
info@re4a.com
www.re4a.com

Roger Hirsch, Myriam Corti
91 Crosby Street, New York,
NY 10012, USA
T: +1 212 219 2609
F: +1 212 219 2767
rhirschny@aol.com

Samuel Lerch
Eibenstr. 9, Zurich 8045, Switzerland
T: +41 1 382 4655
samnad@swissonline.ch

Sandra Aparicio + Forteza Carbonell Associats
Marià Aguiló 1-3, local 5,
08005 Barcelona, Spain
T: +34 93 307 6501
F: +34 93 307 6501
www.fortezacarbonell.com

Smith and Thompson Architects
501 West 26th Street, New York,
NY 10011, USA
T: +1 212 924 4358
F: +1 212 924 8917
smithth1@aol.com

tele-design
2-12-5 Mita, Minato-Ku, Tokyo, Japan
T: +81 3 3769 0833
F: +81 3 3769 9893
tele-web@tele-design.net
www.tele-design.net

Tom McCallum, Shania Shegedyn
shaniashegedyn@bigpond.com

Vicens + Ramos
Barquillo 29, 2° izqda., 28004 Madrid, Spain
T: +34 91 521 0004
F: +34 91 521 6550
vicensramos@arquired.es

Wood + Zapata
444 Broadway, 3rd floor, New York,
NY 10013, USA
T: +1 212-966-9292
F: +1 212-966-9242
www.wood-zapata.com

Yasushi Ikeda, Akiko Kokubun / IKDS
3-10-1 Aobadai, Meguroku,
Tokyo, Japan
T: +81 3 3461 3327
www.ik-ds.com

Ziba Khalili
307 East 89th Street Suite 4G, New York,
NY 10128, USA
T: +1 212 860 0112
F: +1 212 831 2859